FACTS THAT
UNDERGIRD LIFE

Paul Scherer

FACTS THAT UNDERGIRD LIFE

Harper & Brothers Publishers

New York and London

1938

FACTS THAT UNDERGIRD LIFE

Quod latet arcana enarrabile fibra Persius

CONTENTS

SPEAKING OF LIFE

LIFE AS MYSTERY

*The wind bloweth where it listeth, and thou hearest the
sound thereof, but canst not tell whence it cometh, and
whither it goeth. . . .*

JOHN 3:8

"THE most beautiful thing we can experience," writes Albert
Einstein, "is the mysterious"; and nobody I suppose will question his right to speak, as he calls back to us from where he stands
and tries to tell us what he sees. "The man to whom this emotion
is a stranger," he goes on, with the hush in his voice, "the man who
can no longer pause to wonder and stand rapt in awe, is as good
as dead; his eyes are closed." Such a one came to Jesus one night
under the falling shadows in the ancient city of Jerusalem. And
Jesus, with a finger to his lips, spoke softly of the wind stirring in
the tree-tops, how it blows where it will, and one hears the sound
of it, but cannot tell whence it cometh, and whither it goeth. Since
then, among other things, we have made a study of the wind. No
sooner does it begin to tiptoe through the forest, setting all the leaves
of the poplar agog with the witchery of its whispered confidence,
than somebody from the United States Weather Bureau shatters
our dreams by calling for an anemometer to measure its velocity.
Then, what with geodetics and barometrics, he tells us exactly
where it comes from, and in tomorrow morning's paper, in the upper
right-hand corner, exactly where it's going—maybe! It's very distressing, how much we know about everything!

Nicodemus knew too much. That's apparent to anybody who
reads the story there in the third chapter of St. John. He was an
expert. His specialty was religion, and he thought he knew all
there was to know about it. He knew just what kind of person he
was supposed to be. He had read about it in the books. As regards
the technique of getting there, on that he was exceedingly well-
posted. The very first words he uttered were "Rabbi, we know . . ."
If you will follow it through after that you will find how necessary
Jesus thought it was to shatter that false sense of security, that illusion of certainty, that self-complacent smugness, into which this
"ruler of the Jews" had fallen with his knapsack of knowledge.

3

One bewilderment follows another, until the climax of them all is reached in that gentle bit of irony: "Art thou a master in Israel, and knowest not these things?" From that day on Nicodemus knew less and wondered more, while the mastery of a radiant life resolved itself before his eyes into the mystery of a cross and an empty tomb.

Perhaps we shall not be putting an undue strain on anybody's imagination if we take him as the symbol of a generation like ours, whose "forte is science, its folly omniscience," and the expert is abroad in the land. There *is* such a thing—and we are rapidly becoming more and more familiar with it—as Life that has lost all its gracious sense of mystery in the conceit of understanding: its eyes no longer stare anywhere in awe; they look through narrowed slits knowingly. Its head is no longer bowed, trembling with bated breath at the consciousness of Someone's Presence just there and through here: it walks with face straight on and stolid, elbowing its way past a thousand little shrines, and setting its feet unmoved on whatever of beauty it can strip from the earth. For it the age of miracles is past, and there is no wonder in its soul. It has come to think of itself as an incident in the long process of the years, and an almost unspeakably insignificant incident at that, "not only a complete illusion or mirage," in the words of Theodore Dreiser, "which changes and so eludes one at every point, but the most amazing fanfare of purely temporary and in the main clownish and ever ridiculous interests that it has ever been my lot to witness—interests which concern at best the maintenance here of innumerable self-centered and cruel organisms whose single and especial business it is to exist each at the expense of the other—if it were only by cutting each other's hair, and no more!" It has come to suspect that God, and consciousness, and immortality are nothing but the whims of some wishful thinker. It looks at the earth and sees how that was built. It glances up at the stars, and talks wisely of their ages. To everything it doesn't understand it assigns a name, and nods so solemnly that simpler folk mistake its vocabulary for an explanation!

Ours is a hard age for poets. People's eyes used to be wide open in amazement at Life. Now that we are thoroughly sophisticated we look at it with a kind of back-stairs squint—like the parlour-maid's when she's seeing what there is to see!

> "Twinkle, twinkle, little star,
> We know exactly what you are:
> You're just combusting so much mass
> Of C and N and hydrogen gas."

Poetry has its difficulties under the circumstances; and so has religion, and everything else that's outside the realm of our God-forsaken knowledge!—like the

> "Flower in the crannied wall,
> I pluck you out of the crannies,
> I hold you here, root and all, in my hand,
> Little flower—but if I could understand
> What you are, root and all, and all in all,
> I should know what God and man is."

I can't tell how it is with you; but I am thirsty—my lips are dry and parched, for one long, deep, cool draught of ignorance, to help wash down this arid desert of analysis and statistics which I am supposed to swallow and call it knowledge! Wrote the deep, wistful soul of Walt Whitman:

> "When I heard the learn'd astronomer;
> When the proofs, the figures, were arranged in columns before
>   me;
> When I was shown the charts and the diagrams, to add, divide,
>   and measure them;
> When I sitting heard the astronomer where he lectured with
>   much applause in the lecture room,
> How soon, unaccountable, I became tired and sick;
> Till, rising and gliding out, I wandered off by myself,
> In the mystical moist night air, and from time to time
> Look'd up in perfect silence at the stars."

"The wind bloweth where it listeth, and thou hearest the sound thereof, but canst not tell whence it cometh, and whither it goeth." Let's give the lie to it if we can, with our Weather Bureau reports; but there is something in that mood we need to recover. There is no complacent smugness about it, as one should say, "You, my dear man, are nothing but a diversified arrangement of electrons, protons, and quantums." It isn't strutting about with its hat on and a knowing look in its eye, as though Life were as profane as a market-place; it has taken off its shoes, and goes softly on holy ground. And well it may.

For Life holds her mysteries still, in spite of all this drawing up of our chairs, this sitting down so familiarly in front of her—mystery never repellent, always beckoning, like the veils that women used to wear over their faces in the East—like the magic of the mist on land and water—like the gesture and finger of God, with its silent summons,

> "Till at some sudden turn one sees
> Against the black and muttering trees
> His altar, wonderfully white,
> Among the Forests of the Night."[1]

Charles Morgan has put it on the lips of Narwitz in "The Fountain": "What we have hitherto called omniscience is better thought of as an infinite power of wonder. Knowledge is static, a stone in the stream; but wonder is the stream itself—in common men a trickle clouded by doubt, in poets and saints a sparkling rivulet, in God a mighty river bearing the whole commerce of the divine mind. Is it not true that even on earth, as knowledge increases, wonder deepens?"

It proved so certainly with that eminent psychologist, William MacDougall, one time of Harvard. Listen to what he says of his own progress from scepticism to religion: "Deserving of the first place in this record of a sceptic's progress is my increasingly vivid realization that in spite of all the splendid achievements of modern science we still live surrounded on every hand by mysteries. On the frontiers of Thought we look out into infinite distances where all is dim and uncertain, where there loom up questions with which we vainly struggle."

No, it isn't knowledge that banishes God, it's the conceit of it; it's this scientific *Babbittry*, with never in its busy, noisy days a worshipful silence, nor anywhere on its barren landscape a place to kneel and hear the sweep of wings and feel the fleeting touch of a cool hand like the peace of God. It's blindness to all that's beyond our knowing, beyond the wind and the flower and the sunset and little children—deafness to One Who utters Himself in "the special countenance of every season, in fragrant names and city streets, in

[1] Collected poems of Rupert Brooke. Dodd, Mead & Co.

dripping eaves and the homely facts of houses where men and women live, in the color of words and the beat of rhythm," in birth and death and "the salt smell of the deep."

Life holds her mysteries still; and when I turn from that world without to this world within I am face to face with the greater mystery of my own selfhood, lifting up its head with a strange sense of its high inheritance, and in the redeeming fellowship of a Nazarene setting its feet steadfastly toward a glory that both daunts it and cries it on. When George Mallory was telling his American audiences in 1922 why he had already taken part in two attempts to scale Mount Everest, and was about to set out a third time, he said to them: "If you cannot understand that there is something in man which responds to the challenge of this mountain and goes out to meet it, that the struggle of life itself is upward and ever upward, then you won't see why we go."

"Nothing but an arrangement of electrons, protons, and quantums." You can't hold that over me now. There are depths it can never plumb, and heights unexplained where my hands reach out toward the crystal beauty of a life Galilean and God-like. A human soul in the cleansing, lifting grip of Christ; and you and I still strutting about with our hats on, and a knowing look in our eyes? No mystery left? Down all the ways of life with the Spirit of God brooding over them? While there before us wait the victories that God can win with these poor lives of ours! Mystery? "Didn't a certain black friar one day," writes another, "open his heart to a youth? He is forgotten, and yet he made Scotland; for his words gripped and haunted John Knox! And didn't a disappointed man in an Argyle-shire glen, with nothing to encourage him, keep on teaching his dwindling class year in, year out? And have not the ends of the earth good cause to honor him? Because one day a little lad, as he sat there and listened, made up his mind to be what he became, James Chalmers of New Guinea, whom Stevenson so envied?"

"The wind bloweth where it listeth, and thou hearest the sound thereof, but canst not tell whence it cometh and whither it goeth." Yes, Nicodemus knew too much, or thought he did—until Christ found him and took him like a wondering child to the sea again, through long corridors in the Father's House that were new to him, and great, wide rooms where he had never been. Come, give Him your hand: it's for you too, this mystery of life—a worshipping soul before God, and all that may be!

THE GLORY OF THE UNCONSIDERED

*O Lord, open thou my lips; and my mouth shall shew
forth thy praise.*

PSALM 51:15

THE fifteenth verse of the 51st Psalm introduces us to a man who has just one reason at the moment for wanting to speak: he wants to praise God. He doesn't want to complain about anything just now, or—as we say—"bless anybody out"; or address the neighbors on the Tendencies and Perils of our Time. He doesn't want to debate the Supreme Court Issue or advise stockholders or question the Labor Party. He simply wants to say—well, that God is a great God and that his mercy endureth forever. He wants to say that the earth is the Lord's and the fulness thereof. That's the way he feels. He wants to say as solemnly as he knows how that it's good—night and day and changing season, storm and laughter and tears. He wants to hold up in grateful memory, as with hands of thanksgiving, firesides and shadows, the shouts of children, friendships, a stranger's voice, even the wounds and hurt and bitter experience which have made him strong and sunk his roots deeper than a tree's. With plenty of material for a book of Lamentations, he chooses a *Te Deum!*

And I think I understand his mood. He has grown suddenly conscious, as one does at times, of all the unconsidered glory of the world. The cleansing power of God, that unspeakably rich and gracious thing, has swept like a tide through the narrow straits and inlets of his soul, and all around him there begins to sound again in his ears the sober, stately music of life—a music that is quite independent of his circumstances. This song will be on his lips now in spite of everything. So has it always been with God's redeemed.

There is a deeply moving story of those, long after him, whom Rome condemned—dragging them for the name of Christ to the galleys and then in chains to the iron mines of Africa, branding them on the brow, as likely as not gouging out an eye, and sending them down with a lamp and a mallet forever. But there on the walls they left the record of their own slow death in a single word that runs like a kind of frenzy through all their inscriptions: Vita, they wrote—Life; Vita, Vita, Vita—over and over again in long black

8

lines as swallows fly chasing one another toward the light. And they didn't mean they hoped for it; they meant they had it—life, in the damp and the dark—abundant life, in Christ Jesus. Theirs was a tragic hymn, from the bowels of the earth; but like the Psalmist's it was praise!

My suggestion here is that—quite to the contrary—you and I, who are comparatively undemonstrative folk, go about in our world overlooking occasions for thanksgiving. We have almost made it a business, so wary have we grown of life, so cautious and unconvinced of any good. We don't intend to poke our noses in and out of a pretty tough existence, like Pollyanna, hunting for things to be glad about! All right. I agree. Let's not hunt. I'm as suspicious as you are of the chap who is always turning things over and feeling them to see if he can't find a blessing somewhere. If you break your leg he says you should be glad it wasn't your neck. Sure! You ought to be very glad it wasn't a score of things, from a bank-robbery to shipwreck. But you are none the less sorry you broke your leg!

It seems to me there is something obnoxious and offensive about this idea that you have to institute a search all up and down and across every misfortune to discover Santa Claus in it. A misfortune is a misfortune, as I see it, and there's no use being glad that it isn't some other misfortune. Good may come of it, yes. Not a doubt of that. You can whip a dozen misfortunes into shape by the grace of God and make them sing like a choir together! But the secret of a genuinely grateful heart lies in the recognition of common mercies, mercies you don't have to look for as if they were hard to find, hidden away under a rubbish-heap of useless, painful things; you just open your eyes one day and see them. They have been there all along, thank the Good Lord and Sire of every unconsidered grace! We haven't stopped long enough to be aware of them, that's all. Just as we don't stop long enough to be aware of the good in people, but flare out angrily at some irritating surface wrong. We don't stop, and we miss the best of those we love; and we miss God!

I guess it was because nobody in Paris would stop and look that Jean Baptiste Pierre Lamarck day after day lay on the floor of his windowless garret, with no overcoat, and through the skylight studied the clouds. You may still read his descriptions of what he saw; the rare formations that anyone might have seen but no one did. He had found for the science of generations to come his deathless bit of the glory of the unconsidered.

And I suppose it was because men always had glanced at the birds and beasts of the forest without ever stopping long enough to see them that a young lad, broken in fortune, set out with his wife into the Kentucky wilderness singing to it, playing to it on his violin, watching it, and leaving to the future its shy creatures painted as in life on the pages of his album, signed with his name, John James Audubon. He too had made his glad pilgrimage into the glory of the unconsidered.

And let me say this; it's important: this glory of the unconsidered takes up more room, when you come actually to think of it, than anything else in the world. These things to which we scarcely, if ever, give a thought, not only make up the bulk of life, they are the real wealth of it.

Consider, for example, the interesting case of the self-made man. He will tell you that he had no decent start, he had no decent schooling, he had no decent assistance along the way; but look at him now. He's dictating to his own stenographers and riding home behind his own chauffeur. And he has nobody to thank but himself! God pity him! But that's his story; while all around is this glory of the unconsidered. There was the mother who bore him, and forgot her sorrow for the joy that a man was born into the world. There is the past of human life with all the wealth it has won for him, and the present of laboring hands that harvest his wheat and weave his cloth and build his home and print his books and guard his sleep. You may look at him from morning to night and nothing that you see will be very important. All that's really important—one is sorely tempted to say it—lies behind the scenes of the little stage he has built to strut on—a glory quite forgotten, but filling the whole earth, red with the death of martyrs, alive with the noise of ships and the patient murmur of ten thousand men.

Or take your own weeks and months and years and tell me what has happened to them of late—what failures, what burdens, what victories, what friends. When your careful inventory is complete, I wager you that you will have recorded no more than a puny fraction of the whole. Around all you can remember, these things which you think and say are your life—around them, as if they were tiny boats on an untravelled sea, stretches the incalculable goodness of God:

memories, the beauty of the earth, hurts healed, this painless breath, love, a star reflected in water, music. You can't even begin to get your bearings in that uncharted vastness. And then you talk about this and that which didn't go as you had planned. You there, in the midst of all that He could think of and you've forgotten! The ocean of God's love which bears up the little islands of our pain!

Now I want to point all this today with just one solitary unremembered kindness of *Le Bon Seigneur*. I like that Feudal French—"the good Sir Knight and Lord." The kindness he has done us in the gift alone and deep mystery of speech! Simply to say out loud the names you love, the hopes and fears and faith and all the dear nonsense of a day! Never in your life have you thanked God for that. You never thought.

Perhaps that's why we have grown used to speaking so carelessly to one another, and cheaply sometimes, as if on this point at least we need not concern ourselves overmuch. Words, we say, are such usual things, such casual, futile things; it doesn't matter much what we do with them or to what level we let them sink. Let them be frivolous or bitter or indifferent or vulgar—they're only words. It's deeds that count!

Dr. George Buttrick recalls a day when he sat at a high school commencement staring at that motto in huge letters above the platform: "Deeds, not words." And he was in an agony to set it right. For of course words are deeds—tremendous, potent deeds—that turn the tides of history, shatter human lives, paint pictures, carve motives, light lamps. And we deal carelessly with them! Why, all the great business of the Gospel is with words! Without them not even the loving-kindness of Jesus could have survived the hammer and the nails. All that he did would have died, had not some man's words— a Matthew's, or a Luke's—come running to clothe it with life forever!

And we deal carelessly with words! Well, there stands this warning against it: Verily, verily, I say unto you, every idle word that men shall speak, they shall give account thereof in the day of judgment. Precisely because words are never idle. They carry the sorrows and the joys, the duties and the burdens of the world on their back. I've loved them ever since I can remember, the sound and color and fire of them; I think I stand in awe of them now, and pray God to help me load them rightly with mercy and some loving kindness!

Listen to me. Let's never cheapen or warp life with words any more, wounding people, battering shy folks back under cover simply because we have more words than they have or know how to use them better, pulling down the few brave flags they have tried to nail fast in the uncertain fight—not that, when with them we can bring God's cheer into whipped lives and the very strength of his arm to those who keep longing and reaching and slipping and praying again, like you!

I suppose we have to have critics, sharp fellows with a sting, just as we have to have mosquitoes. Speech now and then must be given an edge, no doubt. But closer than any critic to the truth was he who said, Be kind; for every man you meet is waging a desperate battle. I think, ultimately, that's what words are for.

Thornton Wilder in one of his three-minute plays tells of a man who stood one day by the pool of Bethesda waiting for the water to be troubled that he might be made whole again. To him the angel came and said, "Stand back. Healing is not for you. Without your wound, where would your power be that sends your low voice trembling into the hearts of men? We ourselves, the very angels of God in heaven, cannot persuade the wretched and blundering children of earth as can one human being broken on the wheels of living. In love's service only wounded soldiers will do." And so, as once more he turned aside, still with his wound, another who had been lame came swiftly from the pool and seeing him stopped short and said, his face clouding over as if suddenly remembering some ancient sorrow, "Come home with me, I pray you. My son is lost in dark thoughts. I cannot understand him. Only you have ever lifted his mood. And my daughter, since her child died, sits in the shadow and will not listen to us. Come with me just an hour."

Is that what wounds are for, and words? For healing and for peace?

NEVER FEAR TO LIVE

Then drew near unto him all the publicans and sinners for to hear him.

LUKE XV:I

WHAT I want you to notice about these people particularly is that they were of all people in that first-century society the most dismayed. They were beset by a thousand fears. The publicans, who collected the taxes from their own countrymen, were despised and harassed as traitors; the sinners, who had broken the law, were snubbed and kicked into a corner. Both classes had to eke out their poor existence in the face of a world that was always hostile and always threatening. And Jesus deliberately set about helping them. He tried to make things different for them. It grew into a passion with him. Smug Pharisees and complacent scribes would have to take care of themselves. Nothing had happened to them. These others were hurt. Life had done something to them. You could see it in their eyes, shifting and uneasy. They wouldn't look at you. They made you think of hunted animals. It was as though some strange fear had got them down. Some of them were just the more or less blameless, because unthinking victims of circumstance, like the lost coin; others had wandered off on the spur of the moment, following some vagrant impulse, like the lost sheep, that never meant to be wicked—any sheep's face will tell you that—but simply nibbled away after its own desires impromptu! And now they were apprehensive, and restless, and fidgety; they were shaky, and timid, and faint hearted. So he told them these stories of a loving, seeking, restoring God. There was no need to be despondent or anxious any more. There was room for them and as good a chance as any man had. Life was still there with all its amazing possibilities unprejudiced and unhurt: let them march out like free souls in the grace of God, clear-eyed and straight, and take possession of it! And from that day to this the Gospel of Jesus has meant more than anything else good news for people who are full of misgiving, who for one reason or another are daunted and discouraged and afraid to live!

To a greater or less degree, I suppose, that's pretty much the case with all of us. Some people are more afraid to live than to die; that's

why they take their own lives! We begin I think by being afraid of
life as fate. Things happen through no fault of ours. We save money
and the bank fails. We take up some profession and lose our health.
We learn to be telephone operators, and the dialing machine comes
along and throws us out of a job. We build our lives around some
other person, and that person dies. It's all a hazard and a gamble
and a risk. We wonder sometimes if a man can be equal to it. All
around us on the streets, in breadlines, in hospitals, in poverty-
stricken homes, are men and women who haven't been able to keep
on their feet. Maybe it will be our turn soon, and we'll drop out of
the picture just as they have, like somebody's dime rolled off into a
dusty crack. It's a way life has, turning careless and cruel like that,
and leaving us stranded: sometimes it just seems to be a man's fate,
and nobody at all to blame!

At other times, as we look back, we realize that the fault has been
our own: we made mistakes. They were quite inadvertent mistakes,
but no matter; the result is the same. We showed poor judgment.
We did something in ignorance. We acted without thinking really.
There were two roads to take and we took the wrong one. None of it
was intentional. Our consciences are absolutely clear on that point.
But what good is it? The upshot of the whole matter is only a little
less bad than if we had been guilty! At any rate, that's how it feels.
If you're lost, out in the wilderness somewhere, the effect is just
about the same for an innocent sheep as it is for a wilful goat! People
pay for their mistakes, and that makes us afraid. God knows what
the future will be!—with you and me here blundering into it—
blundering even at our best!

"Then drew near unto him all the publicans and sinners for to
hear him." We want to know what message this Man has for
daunted lives. Here is a brave woman's message. I came across it
the other day. This is what she says: "I should never have started to
write if I had not been paralyzed down one side for three years, and
unable to do anything but write. I should never have learned to walk
again if I had not formed the habit of rolling out of bed whenever I
was left alone, hanging on to the foot rail with one hand, dragging
myself up, and dragging myself along it, for what seemed like miles,
until I got to the end. And I should never have done the most exciting thing I ever did in my life if I had not been told that I would
never get well again, and so bundled myself off on a sailing ship.

They said I should never be out in the hot sun, or chance getting a chill, or eat meat, or drink coffee. Yet I slept on deck of necessity, until I was blistered by the sun. For breakfast, dinner, and supper I had salt beef or salt pork, fried potatoes, and black coffee. And I was never so well in my life! When I look back there is not a single misfortune or privation or discomfort I would cut out, for by doing so I should destroy part of the pattern and very structure of my life." And then she closes with what the French soldiers used to say during the war:

"You may be mobilized or you may not be mobilized. If you are not mobilized nothing matters; if you are mobilized one of two things happens. Either you are sent up to the front or you are not sent up to the front. If you are not sent up to the front nothing matters; if you are sent up to the front one of two things happens. You are sent into the firing line or you are not sent into the firing line. If you are not sent into the firing line nothing matters; if you are sent into the firing line one of two things happens; you are hit or you are not hit. If you are not hit nothing matters; if you are hit one of two things happens; you are dangerously wounded or you are not dangerously wounded. If you are not dangerously wounded nothing matters. If you are dangerously wounded one of two things happens; you die or you do not die. If you do not die nothing matters. If you die nothing matters."

Well, that's about everything a man has if you leave out religion. It's a kind of Christian stoic philosophy for folk who are full of misgivings. And it's stalwart. I wish we could manage it. There's a far better chance ahead than you figure. That's what she means. It's silly to be afraid. Very few things are going to turn out as you think. If you don't believe it, keep a book and check them. Those that do, if you're the right sort, you can work into your life as a veritable enrichment of its pattern. So wrote Elinor Mordaunt out of her own experience.

But Jesus wasn't satisfied with that. To these lives that were dismayed he talked not of stoicism but of God. He said that life wasn't malicious, and it wasn't careless. Back of it and through it was eternal love, not watching and pitying, like Maeterlinck's God—but willing and seeking. In the day of Coolidge prosperity, with the empire of Mr. Insull at its height, you could forget that love, and say of it jauntily with a certain professor in one of our leading universities: "There is absolutely no reason to doubt that man is capable of going on happily and sanely without any sense of dependence upon God, and without any apprehension of cosmic support." But when all such days should pass, as indeed now they have, then Jesus knew it would be that love, and that love only, which in the ruin of a man's life could find the man, and build him a home again! "Which of you, having a hundred sheep, if he lose one of them, doth not leave the ninety and nine in the wilderness, and go after that which is lost, until he find it?" It's one thing to stand trembling before the wreck of all your hopes in a world where "man's life has no more meaning than that of the humblest insect which crawls from one annihilation to another"; it's an entirely different thing to stand in front of that wreckage in a world where God is walking, whispering old things our hearts heard long since, singing old songs our youth knew!

Dr. Joseph Fort Newton tells a true story of the history of Tennessee. An Indian band had raided a pioneer settlement, and after murdering nearly everybody had carried off some little boys with them into the forest. Years passed, and in a skirmish with the Indians some of their warriors were taken prisoners, among them a few men with faces almost white. Two of the mothers came to see if they could find their lost boys. They walked along the line peering into the wild faces in vain. Suddenly an officer asked if they remembered any melody they used to sing to the boys in days of old. And one of the mothers began singing a crooning lullaby. The effect was startling. All at once a stalwart figure broke from the line and came cautiously toward her. They looked at one another for an instant, she still singing, until the wild man fell on her shoulders and cried for joy.

If that's what the world's like, Someone walking along the line, bringing love back, and dreams on the wings of a song—then there is no fear. "Either what woman having ten pieces of silver, if she lose one piece doth not light a candle, and sweep the house, and seek diligently till she find it?" What is there left then, in all this world, to be afraid of? Certainly no blind fate that overtakes a man and leaves him stranded, like a dime in a dusty crack.

And so, as he went on speaking that morning, the future came alive in their eyes. He saw it, and the joy of it must have been like the joy of the angels of God—to see hope born that way, as though a hand had swept over their faces changing them. They drew nearer, and he smiled. It reminded him of the day in Nazareth when the younger son of the old farmer came home. He told them of it: the father who had waited so long every evening as twilight fell, and the neighbors who shook their heads as they passed in the dusk. And then of how after years of it the little town was all agog one night. Somebody had seen the lone, silent watcher throw open the gate, and uttering a weird cry run into the arms of a ragged tramp all dusty from the road. And now the house was full of lights and hurrying figures. He said something like that was going on in heaven, and they would find themselves, these restless, timid folk, at home again, for all the sorrows they had known, and the pain, and the loneliness; and they would be better for it, and richer, and more themselves.

I would not have my life be one of bliss,
Untouched by heartache, agony, despair—
A pale, anemic thing. My nightly prayer
Is that with each new day I shall not miss
High venturings, nor undeserve the hiss
Of envious human moles who never dare
To touch off rockets in their souls and flare
Above their deepening grooves. O grant me this:
That I shall scale life's peaks, explore its glooms,
Know mountained ecstasies, deep-valleyed pains—
That when my last red sands by Time are sieved
And life has struck my sinews from her looms,
I shall have earned three words o'er my remains:
Beside "was born" and "died"—between "he lived"!

GOD'S CHALLENGE TO MAN

*When Jesus then lifted up his eyes, and saw a great
company come unto him, he saith unto Philip,
Whence shall we buy bread, that these may eat? And
this he said to prove him: for he himself knew what
he would do.*

JOHN vi:5,6

LIFE seems to be forever confronting us with unusual situations,
with difficulties and problems and perplexities, and wanting to
know what we mean to do about it. The whole adventure of living
is a kind of eternal challenge which God keeps issuing to man, as
Jesus issues it here to his disciples. That day had been just a day like
every other day, when suddenly they had what must have seemed to
them an impossible embarrassment on their hands, a crowd far bigger
than any poor hospitality of theirs could satisfy; and Christ there,
turning around with that familiar gesture of his, and taking it for
granted that this was their business! How would they manage?

Nobody lives long in this world without discovering that that's
precisely the way things go. We run along happily enough for a
while, busily planning this, and hoping that: when all at once illness, or loneliness, or disappointment, disaster perhaps, death maybe,
cuts sharp across the days—and we've got to meet it somehow. We
can't go crawling away from it! And this Voice, like the Voice of
God—a God who is in it with us, up to the nail-prints!—keeps asking eagerly, "Whence shall we buy bread—How shall we manage?"
Sometimes it happens over great wide areas of human experience,
and we say that the world is in bad shape. Sometimes it happens
within the narrow limits of a single life, and we say that things have
gone but poorly with us: we hardly know which way to turn. How
to face ahead adequately in the teeth of it all? Life's challenge, or
God's challenge, it makes very little difference what you call it. How
a man can meet it: that's what concerns me.

Of course, there are several wrong ways of going about it, you
may be sure of that! To begin with, there are always the people who
don't seem conscious of any special perplexities in the world around
them. They are aware of their own all right, and quite vocally aware.

They speak out loudly enough when any shoe pinches them. But the condition of the poor, and the chaotic inequities of modern society, and the jealousy of nations, and the tragic misery of millions of disadvantaged lives—these things surely are no responsibility of theirs. They are quite certain with Pippa that, "God's in His heaven, all's right with the world!" And while they write, out there a weird host of "man's inhumanities to man" stalks by the window! There is nothing much to be hoped for from them, in our day or in any other! The first quick agony in Jesus' mind was lest these disciples of his should look at the multitude, and shrug their shoulders, and turn away. He put it squarely to them, and he puts it squarely to us. "No dodging now, no trying to sneak around. This is your business"— he said, yours and mine. There is no condition or circumstance on earth that calls for human sympathy and human wisdom and human courage that you can decently side-step any longer! Things won't right themselves. They never have! And things are wrong. Don't shrug, and pass it up. "How shall we manage?" That's first!

Second, there are the people who have an idea that about all they can do is to restate the difficulty and emphasize it like Philip. "Two hundred pennyworth of bread is not sufficient," said he. This certainly is one of our favorite devices. I know of nothing more agreeable to the average taste than to get started enthusiastically on the ills of the twentieth century. There's such a gorgeous expanse there in which a man may roam about holding violent converse with his neighbors, and shaking his head ominously! I know of nothing which seems at first glance more becoming to the serious-minded citizen with a well-developed sense of right and wrong: and I know of nothing more completely fatuous and utterly vain! What in the world is the sense of rehearsing all the hazards on the horizon and underscoring them? Some of us do that all our lives, and we do precious little else! Do it at conferences—in drawing-rooms. We do it with a generous sweep of the arm for public affairs, and we do it with a precise and careful finger for our own more private matters. We want you to know that we are well-acquainted with the obstacles. "Two hundred pennyworth of bread!" Poor Philip! He wasn't unconscious of the problem; but one is almost tempted to say that he might as well have been!—for all the help he was! He was like the Chorus in the ancient Greek tragedies; and so are all his modern progeny. The Chorus never really did anything; it just waited around for the intermissions, and said all the calamities over again in italics; then the honest-to-goodness actors would come back and try to work it out! I never was able to understand how they could put up with that Chorus!

The last of these wrong ways to face whatever challenge Life and God fling at your feet is to take sudden stock of what you have, decide that it isn't enough, and so reach the final conclusion that you are quite helpless. Simon Peter's brother did that. Andrew was his name. He said there was a lad there who had five barley loaves and two small fishes. I wish he had stopped with that. It would have been great just to garner what resources there were, and lay them quietly in the Lord's hands. But he had to spoil it, and show the poverty of his faith and his hope and his courage all in one fell swoop! "But what are they," he added, "among so many?" I have a notion that's largely the trouble with the better type of wrong leaders today: they don't just pass up humanity's wretchedness with a shrug, as if nothing were the matter; and they don't just keep telling it over like a string of beads. They fairly acknowledge that it's their business; they run over their assets hurriedly; and then they spoil it all by turning pessimistic! They dismiss the possibility of ever doing anything about anything. They are as they are. The world is as it is. There will be no change. They haven't enough to work with. They expect disaster. The darkness deepens. The end is not far off. They plod "through the gathering clouds, grim and mute." And I dare say now and then we are all inclined to agree. There isn't a great deal we can do, inside or outside, about any of it, alone, and with what we have. When God flings down his sudden glove, if what we have is all there is, we are likely to make a sorry mess of it. We can't even handle our own difficult selves. But that isn't the place to quit! That's the place to start! There's one undaunted soul in this world! "Jesus—took the loaves."

Let's see now if we can gather together the elements of a proper approach to all of Life's hazards great or small, public or private. And let's go back to the beginning and start with this: that God knows the answer! Do you remember how careful the writer is here to get out in the open on that point? "Jesus saith unto Philip, Whence shall we buy bread, that these may eat? And this he said to prove him: for he himself knew what he would do." Our minds may be befuddled; but there is a mind that isn't! Among all the complexities of modern life, in the midst of all your own uncertain groping, there is a way through, and God knows that way!—and all the yearning and the motions of an Infinite Spirit are making great, wide gestures toward it! Somehow that strengthens me! To come to a place and be conscious once more that beyond and above all my bewilderment there is wisdom serene and eternal—one who, standing on a hill-top, turns back to me a "shining face, and cries the news that all the tangled forest paths do lead into a high-road, and that ahead are great horizons and the splendor of the rising sun."

Dr. Bowie has told of the first and only time he ever saw Mt. Rainier. "Near at hand," he writes, "the foreground was flat and uninspiring; but then looking east I saw a white radiance shining in the sky. Above the range of lesser mountains, above a drifting bank of cloud, the glittering snow-capped cone of the great peak lifted itself, majestic and alone. So unearthly it seemed that for one breath-taking moment it was hard to believe. But as I looked again I knew it was real, and the whole landscape assumed an instant dignity because of that transcendent beauty brooding there." In some such way I too lift my eyes from the flat and confused landscape of my life; and the Eternal is there and it strengthens me! "This he said to prove him: for he himself knew what he would do."

And then surely it's necessary for us to remember that the solution rests not so much on our ability, as on our pliability in the hands of God! Philip thought Christ's question—"Whence shall we buy bread that these may eat?"—was a business proposition, and called for cleverness. But it wasn't a business proposition at all. It wasn't a challenge to human ingenuity. Life rarely if ever is! It was a challenge, or so it turned out, to human obedience! "Jesus said, Make the men sit down." I wish we could get hold of that. Whatever it is we happen to be facing in our own lives or in the world, the issue depends not on our frantic casting about for remedies: the issue depends ultimately on the power of God to lead out in triumph every human life that gives itself eagerly to his guidance! I don't mean that anybody is relieved of the necessity of thinking and choosing and trying; certainly not! But I do mean that one ounce of clear and quick discipleship at the center of disappointment or failure or sorrow or pain, is better than a pound of strategy!

We have blue-prints a-plenty in this gospel, for our own lives and for the Kingdom of God. There is enough knowledge of his will in this world and in your possession to straighten out all the public and private tangles that can be found! Wanted, nothing under heaven but people to do it! They call that over-simplification nowadays, as though the great, complex wrongs of human society would never yield before such simple things as truth, and honesty, and purity, and justice, and mercy! Which is nonsense. The intricacies of modern life, with all its meticulous adjustments, do nothing but hide its thoroughly simple and perfectly straight-forward immoralities! So with you and me. We may pretend to be perplexed; we hardly know which way to turn: but all the while there is this steady compulsion of another will pressing us on in adversity toward faith, in jealousy toward kindliness, and in loneliness toward mercy and peace. The only virtue we lack is obedience! Living isn't easy, facing steadily these days that come moving toward us out of the future; but it doesn't have to be confused, I'm sure of that! With a God who knows the way through and asks of us only that we follow, there isn't much room for bewilderment!

And so at last the miracle! If nothing but a miracle can get us out, and get the world out, why then I think we ought to be easy in our minds! God's used to working miracles when men and women in the middle of their purposes catch sight of his, and cry as they let the rest go, Lord, what wilt thou have me to do? That day in Galilee, when it was evening, so the story runs, they gathered twelve baskets of the fragments which remained. I am not surprised. There's always more than enough, some surplus of bounty, when God sets about seeing human life through! This thing in front of you, this fear, this lot of yours, this failure, this discouragement, this future, whatever it is that keeps staring you out of countenance—face it with him, and it won't even use you up: there will be grace enough left to share, if you'll only garner it somehow, and put it to work! The people I know who have met Life's hazards with Christ never do seem burned out and exhausted: they had courage enough once; now they have courage enough, and faith enough, to give away! It's no bare victory that's ahead: it's victory with a margin greater than all you had at the start!

Shall we take up then this challenge or that, whatever it is, and do it this day with confidence? Do you remember Peary's words, as after many failures he sat writing on the eve of his final and successful journey to the Pole: "Through all my seasons of disappointment and defeat I have never for a moment ceased to believe that the great white mystery of the North must one day succumb; standing here with my back to the world and my face toward that mystery, I believe that I shall win in spite of all the powers of darkness and of desolation." If there is anything at all of that spirit in you, when Christ comes upon it he will smile, and nod his head eagerly and fashion a life that

> amid all men shall bear itself thereafter
> Smit with a solemn and a sweet surprise;
> Dumb to their scorn, and turning on their laughter
> Only the dominance of earnest eyes.

MAN'S CHALLENGE TO GOD

Then said the Jews unto him . . .

JOHN viii:52

THESE words occur three times in this chapter. What they said isn't of first importance: only that they kept answering him back, and turning and twisting away, and shaking him off. That's what brings me to my subject.

I have tried to show you all along that life is God's eternal challenge to man. In a sense no less true, man is life's eternal challenge to God. Always confronting him is this creature, always difficult, standing sullenly apart from his purpose, striding brazenly across it, running stubbornly against it: a creature whom we are to understand God fashioned in his own amazing image! A few years ago on the stage "Green Pastures" told the story simply and humanly: God with his first high hopes vaguely disturbed, looking down out of his heaven, shaking his head pitifully—sending a prophet, sending a judge, sending a priest—trying to do something as the noise on earth grew louder and more rebellious; at last whispering to himself, as the curtain fell, about a sacrifice which seemed even to him appalling! We have been looking at that long story all our lives from our point of view, watching "the dumb red horror on the world's great altar-stairs," wondering if man will ever find his way to God. It may not be amiss to think of it one day from God's point of view, and wonder if God will ever find his way to man! He has set himself long since to do that, taking human wilfulness, and human indifference, and human bitterness, as a challenge to his love and his patience and his ingenious bounty—bent on coming in somehow, from above or beneath, going round and breaking through, trying one thing and then another—if only somebody will understand, and nod his head eagerly, and say, "Lord, I see. It's clear now. I'll go. You may count on me." That's really the drama of the ages, when you come stumbling up against things as they are: man the impossible over here, with a very genius for holding God back; and over there God the undiscouraged, meaning eternally to do something about it! That's the true and inside story of your own life! "Then said the Jews unto him . . ."

And so I want to look at one or two of these postures men strike, these moods they fling up in God's way, and then stand there with arms akimbo, hoity-toity, trying to hide behind them, and hold him off, and stay on the other side at a comfortable distance. They are doing it here in this eighth chapter of John. You and I are doing it now in whatever chapter we happen to be writing.

The first challenge which God must get around somehow, or break through, is the eternal challenge of the old. What the Jews couldn't get was that anything had happened which might conceivably make Abraham a little passé, and the prophets, too! "Art thou greater than they?" The Jews kept shouting it at him. "They are dead, and thou sayest, If a man keep my saying he shall never taste of death. Whom makest thou thyself?" The old victories were victories enough. They went strutting about, thumb in arm-hole, showing off their ribbons, sticking out their chests with the medals on them, calling the roll of all the ancient heroes to shame this young Galilean upstart into silence. It was the old order that was God-given. Things were better then. Let a man scuttle back and be saved! Abraham! The prophets! Back, I tell you, get back!—And the past got between them and the future. It got between them and God. They crawled behind it and hid, and grew rigid, and showed their teeth, and spat!

It doesn't require much ingenuity to bring that up to date. Let's clip two pages now out of such history as happens to be in the making. One of the great and momentous things, it seems to me, which in our day God is trying to say to us, is that war is sin. I may be wrong about it. He may look on with approval while his children fall to and kill one another. That may be the "clear Word of God," as the editor of one periodical recently implied. But I don't believe it! And to quote Luther, as this particular editor did, doesn't strike me as being tremendously impressive. It's just another dodge at trying to push life back, and keep it in its ancient moulds, crying forever that what was is God's way, and what is to be is none of his business! Luther's arguments on the subject, by the way, are unfortunately like a sieve for the holes that are in them; but right or wrong I am asked to retreat to them. Just as I am asked by some hundred-per-cent Americans to frown on every attempt at organizing a World Court because George Washington happened to say something one day after lunch about "entangling foreign alliances."

God save us from this pernicious habit of going back, and turning solid, and stuffing our ears full of cotton! Perhaps we are trying to bring about the millennium, as this good editor says, when we talk of doing away with war, of ridding ourselves of the accursed thing anyhow: but so has everybody else in this world who has ever done anything about anything! They have all been trying to bring about the millennium, and even editors may start! We have a certain high example in a man named Jesus! Quit talking about going back— unless: unless you mean going back to the truth. And the truth thus far has proved itself to be pretty well in advance of most of us!

The other page from current history, the other thing, it seems to me, which God is trying to tell us is, that we have to do better with our economic order than we have been doing. Maybe the capitalism of the 'twenties was inspired, with its consistently high price-levels. I doubt it. Maybe every other system is damnable and corrupt. I doubt that. But on one subject I have no doubt at all, and it's this: if you and I don't willingly let go of a few old privileges, and a half-dozen selfish advantages which we have been loath to pass on, we'll be blasted away from them! There was a play downtown not long ago called "Love on the Dole." It was the tragic tale of young life trying to hold on to the crust of living, and watching it crumble. With a situation like that God has nothing to do. And with whatever it is that makes a situation like that not only possible but inevitable, God will not have anything to do long! We ought to have amazingly open minds just now, sane, free of prejudice, eager for adjustment, no matter what it costs us, ready to pour out ourselves and what we have if only the future can be better for it. And let happen what will, for God's sake and humanity's quit holding up the past like some sacred symbol to frighten life back out of that future! There are times when we'd better listen a little more closely to God, and a little less closely, perhaps even to the Constitution— or anything else the old does to us to make us think it will last forever! Believe me, in this place I am no man's advocate, and I am the advocate of no policy, of no order. I am God's advocate, at least I try to be: and I know that he leads us by strange paths sometimes. I know that with his pillar of cloud by day and fire by night we grow out of what has been, and leave it, like Egypt there!

"Then said the Jews unto him . . ." You see, they dared him to do anything with them. The past was enough. They wouldn't budge.

And God took up their challenge. He always does. He took up their challenge with life, moving, thrusting, jostling life, and it swept by them! It swept out of the Old Testament into the New. It swept out of the New, holding fast to nothing but the direction it had got in Jesus of Nazareth, its solemn swing Godward! It's sweeping on now, if I may change to a figure I love, like a ship setting her sails to the strong winds with the salt spray at her bow. Your old victories, your old defeats, be they as holy to you as Abraham and the prophets, have slipped out in the wake! Let them go! What's new may not be true. I know that. But this I know, too: that what's old, if it's good, will be still with God, and God's ahead!—meeting with change the challenge of all the old that needs changing! That's the challenge of the old!

The second challenge which men fling out as they try to keep God at a distance is what I shall call the challenge of the outward. I mean by that this plaguing, persistent notion that if we arrange the outside of life so that it looks all right, as we have been trying to do here thus far, why then the inside either doesn't matter, or it will take care of itself. Of course, when you put the matter crudely like that, you see how utterly futile a program it is for any life. It's like treating the symptoms and letting the disease carry on through the body whatever ravages it will, if only you can keep them under some decent cover: doctoring up the sores of smallpox, or prescribing for the headache of a patient with typhoid fever! But that's precisely what we continue to do. The Jews were open and above-board about it. They had a stated ritual of prayers and sacrifices, and if you stuck to that you were all right. Jesus called them whitewashed sepulchres, and said that the faith which didn't issue in love and humility and human brotherhood wasn't worth a great deal. We have been more subtle than the Jews. We have fastened on the good manners of Jesus, on the daily, outward conduct of his life, and made of that— not the issue, as he did, but the essence of religion. We keep playing about with what we think is justice and mercy and the soft answer which turneth away wrath, practising this, modifying that, substituting something else; and we go on wondering what's wrong: because none of it seems to work; there is no fundamental change anywhere. Families that can't seem to get along together scratch their heads in bewilderment and reverse their tactics. They don't reverse themselves. Serious-minded Christians struggle with acid jealousies, or blazing tempers, or melancholy dispositions. Reformers muster all their forces and throw their weight about in the slums. Some of them begin to feel almighty righteous if they can get a bill passed in the legislature. And the only trouble with all of it is that too often we keep standing there in God's face pretty much the same sort of people we were before, except for a few decorative additions we have filched from the Sermon on the Mount!

So it is, says Leslie Weatherhead somewhere, that everything we do, which we believe to be in accordance with God's will, can become a barrier to keep our souls from him: the money we give, the service we render, the kindness we show—a man can hide himself behind it, as the Jews did behind the formalities of their religion, away from the disturbing eyes of Christ, and go to sleep feeling very content in dressing gown and slippers. You can hold up your poor attempts at being good, the zeal you show for righteousness and the Kingdom of God, your growing passion for economic justice and a thirty-hour week—you can hold it all up in front of your conscience while you sneak away on the other side of it as far as ever you can from the vexing, harassing, prodding, uncomfortable reality of God! It's a way life has of avoiding anything that promises to upset it! Standing there in God's face with its little virtues, thinking well of itself. That's man's ultimate challenge to God!

And God took up that challenge on Calvary! The cross, on one of its aspects surely, was Christ's last bid, his final fling, for the whole man—not the outside only, where we do justly, but the inside, too, where we love mercy and walk humbly! God would never be satisfied with less. And so he stood up on a hill one day that shattering thing, to beat down your defenses and mine! The story is told of Thomas Mott Osborne that he began his career by donning prison stripes at Auburn, and living for a while in every detail the life of a convict. One day he was engaged in carrying out some menial and revolting assignment, while a tough and unusually cold-blooded old lag who knew him stood by looking on with a sneer. Gradually, as the younger man kept at it unflinchingly, the sneer began to fade, and something like wonder crept into that hard face. Perhaps the world wasn't as ugly and selfish as it had always seemed. Possibly there was kindliness in it, ready to get down like this under other fellows' burdens. And a lump came up in the old convict's throat, and he turned away as he felt his defences falling, falling. That's how it happens, as Someone gathers his arms full of the unloveliest things on earth and goes staggering with them up a strange hill toward a cross! God thought you would care about that, and instead of just acting differently, would be different. He thought you would see it was you he was after, and you might let him get hold of your life. You wouldn't go priding yourself then on the things you had done, and hiding behind them. You wouldn't go hugging yourself so securely for the figure you had cut. You would give in, that's what; and you wouldn't be worth anything, for the love hanging there; and suddenly you'd be worth the world, because God did that; and the springs of your life would be clean, and they'd start flowing into a river, and maybe rush into a flood, and you would be God's man at last—God's whole man! That I think is the way he planned it, anyhow—that day, so long ago now, when he set out in pursuit of us!

FACTS THAT UNDERGIRD LIFE

The grace of the Lord Jesus Christ, and the love of God, and the communion of the Holy Ghost, be with you all. Amen.

II CORINTHIANS xiii:14

G. K. CHESTERTON once remarked that if you ever happened to find yourself on the point of renting a room from some landlady, you should not ask her first about the food or the sheets or the price of such accommodations as she might be able to offer. It would be far better and more useful, he said, to fix her with a steady eye and put to her severely this question: Madam, what is your total view of the universe? And of course he was right! In the long run everything else turns out to be quite secondary. It's your philosophy of life—what you think of its origin and its purpose and its destiny; what you think of the facts that lie beneath it and the goals that are set for it: all this that's of prime importance; not the making of beds or the frying of bacon or the rendering of bills!

And so I offer no apology for attempting to set before you the three basic conceptions which have upheld now for twenty centuries the life of the Christian community. Paul records them in the so-called New Testament benediction, which is a sort of threefold idea of God held in solution, not crystallized yet into any doctrine, with no effort at definition, just the bare statement of an experience which any man may have of the grace of our Lord Jesus Christ, and the love of God, and the communion of the Holy Ghost; not an abstruse philosophy, out of touch with life; not simply a revelation, to be received on the authority of a book and recited in a creed: but an insight; an insight into the nature of that ultimate reality which undergirds the universe; a judgment of essential values—values inherent in the very process of living, values without which life cannot continue long or prove valiant and victorious. This that we call today the doctrine of the Trinity is really just a home-body bit of philosophy in its over-alls! I want you to watch it at work.

And I am going to begin where Paul begins, with the grace of our Lord Jesus Christ. In the New Testament, grace means more than charm and winsomeness; it means the sum total of all the blessing

which Jesus came to bring and to be. It means mercy and truth.
It means the divine favor. It means the power of God—resting now
by reason of a Galilean upon human life. And all this in order that
every man might at last discover himself to be a creature of the most
amazing capacities, intrinsically great, and potentially triumphant.
This surely is what Christ has wrought on the stage of the world.
It's all that he has wrought, when you come to draw a line under
it and add it up. He has brought everlastingly into the foreground
of human thought the central, redeemed, abiding dignity of the
human soul!

There is an ancient legend which tells of the day when men first
stood before the gods daring to be like them, sensing within themselves a kinship which made them walk a little more proudly on the
earth. But the gods in their jealousy stole that spark of their own
life away, and sought to hide it out of all sight and reach. Weeks
passed into months, and in their counsels no place for it was found.
For man ranged the mountains and plumbed the seas and peered
inquiringly into the heavens. Nowhere would the spark be safe.
Until at last the great god Brahm took it in his hands and gave signal
in the long hall for peace. Briefly he vanished—and was back again.
There was a smile now on his face. "Fear not," he said; "I have
hidden the spark where man will never in all his days think to
search. I have hidden it securely in his own heart!"

Jesus of Nazareth had nothing to do with the hiding of that spark:
everything that he was and did served to reveal it. Men began to
think of themselves differently because he had come. They grew
very certain that for all their poor and seeming estate, for all their
persistent cheapness and poverty, they did amount to something, and
could amount to more. You could call them fools if you liked. And
maybe they were. You could watch their deliberate deviltry, and
their tragic mistakes, and throw up your hands in despair. You could
make up your mind that humanity was crazy, and needed to be put
in a strait-jacket, with some Stalin cracking his whip over it, or
some Hitler, or some Mussolini. But all the while—deep under its
wilfulness and its folly was still that divine possibility, that god-like
capacity for some grace of being finer than itself. Because Christ had
lived, and guaranteed it with the death he was willing to die! You
needn't be discouraged any longer about human nature if you didn't
want to be. He wasn't. You could run a heavy line through all

your cynicisms. And when things seemed blackest, you could gird yourself for some new triumph—though you might not know just what—of the human spirit! There was something intrinsically great about the soul, and potentially triumphant!

And we are getting hold of that. Surely we are. This short record of the Saviour's life, comprising as it does the scattered words and events of not more than a hundred days, perhaps not more than sixty, has so tied and twisted itself into the mind of the twentieth century that we cannot long think meanly of each other. I know—there are whole battalions of books written about our puny stature and our miserable stupidity. Now and then somebody lets out a blast and calls us apes. But we don't act on any of it. We listen to the wise men who run down our feckless, silly selves, and we nod very soberly; because God knows they make out a good case. But then we shake our heads and bite our lips and hitch up our belts and live by Christ's judgment of us, not by theirs! Why that's what our stubborn faith in democracy means. It means that finally we do believe in this stuff we're made of. You may sneer at that faith, but in its stately shadow every man that's worthy of the name has to do his living! Let it slip, and a very hell's broth of trouble begins to brew. Hold it fast, and a glory is born in the earth.

And mark you—It's Jesus of Nazareth and no other, who has snatched to its feet this central gallantry of human life which is the human soul! "The grace of our Lord Jesus Christ." We have to begin with that if we are ever under the sun to get anywhere!

And then we have to assume a universe that back of all its changing moods is friendly. That's the second point. "The grace of our Lord Jesus Christ, and the love of God." There you have it: faith in the endless capacities of the human soul, and faith in the underlying friendliness of the world we live in. There's no doing without that long. Oh, I suppose we can afford a little irreligion on this point as on the other—some few denials, a cackle or two of laughter, and a moderate pile of statistics thrown over against it; but life can't afford a great deal of irreligion on either of them. If the tide of unbelief should ever rise high enough to sweep clean away man's ultimate confidence in man, and his final trust in the essential goodness and meaningfulness of creation—well, I have no doubt we'd still go on talking of life, but after a bit there wouldn't be any that you'd want to buy with a brass farthing!

To build anything long, with any firmness, from a democratic state to a decent home in the country, we've got to assume that this huge order of which we are a part is a big sight more than a half-witted grin on the face of nothing! When Michelangelo used to carve out his statues, he did it in marble; because marble would last. It had some staying qualities. He didn't put together a lot of sand on the sea-shore and spend his talents on that! If this world of ours is just waiting around in circles like an idiot for its doom, if it's positively hostile, or if it's really indifferent to us—then there isn't any great encouragement anywhere, is there, for this indefatigable, undisheartened laborer called man? And he won't stick it forever on such terms! You may be sure of that! Not if he finds out!

The fact is, we live by our faith in the world, and not by our doubts. That's all that saves us. No end of smart people poke fun at the friendliness which we profess to find at the bottom of all created things, as we go about looking for a face, and calling life's deep neighborliness "the love of God!" They poke fun at it; but nobody much pays any attention to them. They insist that human beings are just robots, growing from the inside out, and producing other little robots; but if they themselves should ever come upon such a conception as that in a story book, they would smile and shrug their shoulders and dismiss it as a fantasy! They keep telling us that honor and justice and mercy are so much jargon in a world as unresponsive to such nonsense as a granite hitching-post is to the befuddled hum of insects on a summer's day! But they don't convince many. We go on assuming, most of us, that good lies nearer the heart of the world than evil, and that somehow something is being done about it down here. We skillfully plant that fixed pillar in the chaos—not in any effort to swallow the universe, which would be bad for our logical digestion; but to keep the universe from swallowing us! "The earth is full of the goodness of the Lord." You may say you don't believe that; but you live by it! Because you were born to live by it! And tomorrow morning you'll go ahead and do the best you can on the basis of it, with a strange and haunting suspicion that life matters and you matter and the world does make some sort of permanent sense!

We are told that Goya, the artist, aged and in exile at Bordeaux, would ask people in the cafes to drop three crumbs at random on a piece of paper; and that then, however remote and awkwardly separated these might be, he never failed to draw a figure with its head and hands where the crumbs had been. "The love of God." It's the only thing under heaven that binds all the inconsistencies, the bitter irrelevancies of the world together, and forces them into a single pattern that doesn't offend the mind! And the pattern is a head that's crowned with thorns, and hands with nail-prints in them! So Dante, viewing from the vantage point of eternity his own life of exile and unrelieved misery, calls it a "sweet harmony" played on some mighty organ. And the apostle, looking around on tribulation and distress, on nakedness and famine and peril and persecution and sword, speaks of a "pageant of triumph," and drawing himself up to his full height nails his flag to the mast: "If God be for us, who can be against us? He that spared not his own son, but delivered him up for us all, how shall he not with him also freely give us all things?" "The love of God." That fixed pillar too we must have, or we are no men in a ridiculous world!

And now this other: "the communion of the Holy Ghost." Somewhere near the core and center of that phrase I think is the faith that in this life of ours there is a fellowship with the Spirit of God which among other things keeps all human ideals alive. I know of nothing else that could have done that. You don't need to be told how easily a man can lose all the ideals he ever had. The very passing of the years sometimes is enough of itself to dull their glory. Thousands of them come to nothing—exactly nothing, or so it seems. And almost all the people you meet along the way will tell you how foolish they are. Ideals! Until at last you are willing—or you would be, if there were not Someone abroad who won't let you! —to sit down and counsel all youthful lives everywhere against such folly.

But there is that strange man on a cross and he won't allow it now! Just a handful of people saw him die. Their dreams died with him. Then on a queer day, with what seemed like the sound of a rushing, mighty wind, the dreams were alive again! It wasn't simply that hope springs eternal in the human breast. Peter at least was confident that much more was going on than that. "This it is," said he, "which was spoken by the prophet Joel; and it shall come to pass in the last days, saith God, I will pour out of my Spirit upon all flesh; and your sons and your daughters shall prophesy, and

your young men"—no longer living, as young men do in the present
—"shall see visions, and your old men"—no longer living, as old
men do, in the past—"shall dream dreams."

I do not believe that since then humanity could have stood alone
and held on to its dreams if God had left it to itself. You couldn't
have stood alone if God had left you! There have been too many
disappointments, too many wretched disillusionments along the
road, for anybody to suppose now without God that there is anything in dreams. I heard of one disillusionment not long ago, put
with all the bitter irony of life. Dick Sheppard was here,—some of
you will remember his book, "The Impatience of a Parson," and his
great ministry at St. Martin's-in-the-Fields, there on Trafalgar Square
in London; he was here in America and told of a lad who was shot
through the neck in the great war and died in his arms. The last
words the poor chap spoke were about the child his wife was soon
to bear him. "If it's a boy," he whispered, "I'm glad he won't have
to go through this. This is a war—to end war—isn't it?" And Dick
Sheppard comforted him, saying—because he believed it too—"Yes,
Yes,—a war to end war!" Today the child that was born is just
twenty years old, dressed in a soldier's uniform, drilling somewhere
in England! In God's Name, isn't that enough to kill a dream?
And the answer—here is the marvel of all marvels—the answer is
"No!" It's not enough to kill a dream—not while the Spirit of God
is abroad in the earth! We're building yet on this—this off-chance
of God that we are not all going down in foolish ruin. If some of
us do—why then with sweat and tears, the others will build again!
For you see, it isn't the ideal that lives: it's God, and the dream in
his great heart, his dream of the world and of you!

"The grace of our Lord Jesus Christ, the love of God, and the
communion of the Holy Ghost." I wonder if you see any more
clearly now how that ancient doctrine of the Trinity, because it was
first an experience, still conserves and interprets the most immediately
valuable of all the truths that undergird our life: faith through
Christ in the human soul; our belief in a friendly world held fast
in a Father's love; and this knowledge—which no failure can ever
betray—that you and I may turn back now into the thick of things,
and even if the vision tarry, we can wait for it there with quiet eyes;
for it will come: and it will not be late!

THE PERIL AND THE PROMISE OF THE UNUSUAL

Who, when he was reviled, reviled not again; when he suffered, he threatened not.

I PETER ii:23

HERE are some of the things that Jesus did not do. And they must have struck Peter with considerable force: for he remembered, no doubt, James and John; how they had wanted to call down fire from heaven against a churlish village of Samaria, and the soft answer that turned away their wrath. He remembered that evening in the garden, I think, when he himself had drawn his sword and attacked a man with it—how Jesus had rebuked him, and told him to put it up. He remembered the silence of the patient prisoner standing before the court of Pilate, and under the buffeting of the soldiers as they mocked him and spat in his face. He remembered the prayer that went up from the cross while men were cursing and driving nails through flesh. And it all seemed like a weird, intolerable dream to Peter, with the hot blood boiling through his veins. Forty years after it still makes his eyes go wide with amazement, and he sets it down like a man entranced. When he was reviled, reviled not again; when he suffered, threatened not! It was the kind of thing that had a hard time feeling itself at home in this fisherman's rough and ready soul!

But conduct has two sides, as most of us can testify: one is negative, and the other is positive. What Jesus didn't do impressed the aged apostle as being original and unique: there was no resentment, no striking back, none of the violence and bitterness which humanity throws up for a defence when it's hurt. That was one mystery; and all that Jesus did was the other! If ye do well, and suffer for it—so creeps the wonder through his words—a man for conscience toward God to endure grief and take it patiently! After a thousand wayside mercies, with all the truth Jesus had spoken and all the love he had shown, leaving people astonished everywhere—Mark, Peter's pupil, wrote down the marvel of it like an oft-repeated reminiscence. Then to hold your tongue and hold your temper—that was something! And I dare say he shook his grizzled old head: it was difficult to make out. He rings the changes on it all through his letter—until nothing is clearer about Peter than his astonishment at this Christ, the enigma of God!

So you see how one arrives at such a theme. The Peril and Promise of the Unusual. Certainly the life of Jesus is the classical illustration of them both. If he hadn't been so different, on all counts, he could have got away from the world in some safety; but he would never have caught and held its wistful stare for twenty centuries!

That he was different is the ground of the only hope we have. We call him not Jesus the Great: we lift him bodily out of all categories, and call him Christ, the Only. Sonorously in our creeds we recognize the place he holds apart, whose name is above every name, "begotten of his Father before all worlds, God of God, Light of Light, very God of very God." Yet not too far apart. He entered into these lives of ours. He wore them as a man. He wore all of them in their common humanity. And he wore them with a difference. He wore them so that nobody could ever call them ordinary again. He wore them royally, our lives, so that we ourselves might wish, as it were, to touch but the hem of them. They killed him for it. They killed him for being different. But there are millions of people today who are thanking God that he was! It's the peril and the promise of the unusual.

Let's look at the peril first. I don't care who he is, any man who isn't like other men is in danger! And for a very simple reason. There is a useful and necessary tendency in human nature that makes for some kind of conformity. We couldn't live together without it. There are customary reactions to heat and cold, to enmity and friendship, to pleasure and pain. There are habitual processes, and average ambitions, and usual conduct. We are bound to have certain standards in thinking and feeling and practice, or we never should get by without anarchy! And we are bound to conserve them, too, or we should lose most of the value the past has for us. It was a wise dispensation that for our defence against endless confusion enabled us to build up a system of accepted modes and manners, and taught us to look with some suspicion on every breach a man makes in it. Here is half the secret of progress.

But it's only one half: the other half is equally important. If standardization were the last word, life would be static. The nice point lies in knowing just where standardization turns into a liability. That it does, somewhere along the line, is apparent to anybody who gives a moment's thought to it. We standardize our fashions, and become such slaves to the standard that some of us now and then look ridiculous. We standardize our morals somewhere along about the level of the lowest common denominator of the social conscience. There is a standardized way of thinking about the economic situation. There is a standardized way of thinking about war and race relations. And the criterion too often is not what is right but what is convenient. As a result, there are times without end when we standardize evil. Cowper gives us one historical instance:

> Such dupes are men to custom, and so prone
> To reverence what is ancient, and can plead
> A course of long observation for its use,
> That even servitude, the worst of ills,
> Because delivered down from sire to son,
> Is kept and guarded as a sacred thing!

We even standardize our ideals, and wherever the Sermon on the Mount doesn't fit into them we reject it as the impractical dream of a visionary.

So it grows clear enough that the other half of progress consists in knowing where and when to break bounds, and then in doing it! But make no mistake: you'll pay for it if you do, in one way or another. Before life will ever learn what you're driving at, it will smack you, if it can, out of the picture. A great deal would be gained in our day, it seems to me, if you and I instead of being surprised, and hurt, and resentful, would take that for granted. Try standing for a new conscience in modern business; but don't expect to get by unhurt. Try standing for some new measure of brotherhood between the races; but don't expect to get by without having men sneer at you and avoid your company. Try standing for international comity and good will as the best and only protection America needs or can have; but don't expect that you will not have to pay the price. At Riverside Church one evening 200 ministers joined in a covenant of peace, disavowing war and pledging themselves never to support another. One of them from the pulpit told us what it meant. "It means," said he, "jeopardizing our civil rights probably; it means jeopardizing life possibly; it means jeopardizing our position in the Church certainly; it means jeopardizing our nation conceivably, when the time shall come for it to stand up in the Council of Nations and say, 'We of America believe that the people of all the world, and their friendship, are more important than we ourselves!' "

It's the peril of the unusual. Life is afraid of everything that doesn't conform, and slaps at it on a thousand fronts. Can't you and I begin with that, and instead of calling Christ's way visionary, as some of us are inclined to do, because it's bound to hurt, assume that it's going to? He did. He never made discipleship seem easy. There were times when He almost leaned over backward, or so it seems to us, for fear somebody might think it was. He was accustomed to meet all the feverish, unthinking enthusiasm that showed itself, with the most chilling sort of realism. He knew, the world being what it is, that love would have to wear thorns and go about with bare feet!

But He knew that love, with the difference it would make, was the only hope the world had! In the peril was the promise. Will you look at that now for a moment?

Have you ever wondered why, for all the danger connected with it, it was always the unusual that Christ demanded? "What do ye," he asked that solemn day when he was speaking of the pure in heart and the meek—"What do ye more than others?"

The average wouldn't serve, no matter how high it happened to be; because for one thing it would never strike the eye! I am putting it very humanly. He had no such ulterior motive in his mind. It was never his purpose to attract attention by being different. But actually that's what comes of it; and Christianity can't get along without the comment it stirs. If anybody is ever going to desire it, the difference it makes has to be manifest enough for a man to see it! And that's precisely what the average is not! As long as you respond to life's taunts, its disappointments and failures and bereavements, its ideas and moods and aims—as long as you respond to all these things as everyone else responds to them, men and women who haven't the faith that you cherish, or the courage and the hope that ought to thrill a human soul when it knows itself to be standing in the eternal presence and love of God; as long as there's no difference there's no market! In its very essence, Christianity is a religion that's committed and dedicated to making a difference;

and the only blight that can ever settle on it is the blight of the ordinary!

More than that. The average doesn't serve because it soon loses the interest not only of others but even of the man who practises it. I wonder sometimes if that isn't at the root of a good deal of our own boredom. We have an idea that sin is exciting; it never seems to occur to us that goodness is too, when you get it off of its dead level! But you have to do that, or it's no more thrilling than any other routine you can fall into! The man who's given to moderation when it comes to reading the Bible, and going to church, and saying his prayers, and being thoughtful and forgiving and kind, is doomed at the start: he'll stretch himself someday and yawn in the face of it all! But just let him begin somewhere around the circle to leave moderation behind him, and try his hand at being a Christian to some unusual extent—kind where nobody would ever expect kindness; thoughtful where everybody would take for granted his not caring a fig; forgiving where it's not only foolish but dangerous to forgive; generous where somebody is bound to take advantage of his generosity. Let him start doing that at the office, and among his friends, and in his own home: it won't take him long to find out what a fascinating business it is, this being a genuine instead of a make-believe disciple of Jesus Christ!

Do you begin to see now what I mean when I speak of the promise of the unusual? It's the only thing I know which will enlist humanity's interest and your own. And surely it's the only thing that has any lifting power. That's the last reason I have for submitting to you that the average never works. Take these three greatest problems that face the world today: the problem of securing a better distribution of economic privilege; the problem of living together amicably and fairly with other races; and the problem of war. Somebody has to start thinking differently about these things, and acting differently, or life is going to be stuck just where it is; in which case, we may as well chuck our religion and quit talking about the power of Christ to change what we know very well is ours to change! Promise, if there is any, doesn't lie in repeating the old formulas, and handing about the old anodynes to keep our uneasy consciences asleep! Let religion stay out of government; and let government stay out of business, so that everybody can get his— now that the getting offers to be a little better—and business may bless religion, and religion may bless government, and we'll always have wars, forever and ever, world without end. Promise, if there is any, lies in one or two new and consecrated experiments in thinking and practice! And there will always be one less made until you come to make yours! Can you take on a bit of experiment next year somewhere, anywhere at all? Just for the sake of the promise it holds out, never mind the cost?

I think it's a good thing for us that we can count on God's doing it. He'll be unusual. He won't strike an average anywhere, and offer his pardon and himself only to the soul that's up on John's level, for instance, or Matthew's, or down here on the level of Judas. He'll get out of bounds and meet you on any level with his patience and his love, like that father Jesus told of, standing there at the gate with his arms around a tramp, making motions to the servants about a robe and a ring and shoes for those weary feet! He won't be moderate, ever! He left a cross on a hill one day as a symbol of the peril and the promise of all goodness everywhere that's willing to go to extremes! And this fisherman writing, with the wonder in his eyes! Reviled, reviled not again! Suffered, but threatened not!

WITH REGARD TO MYSELF

MODERN MAN'S DILEMMA

He beholdeth himself, and goeth his way, and straightway forgetteth what manner of man he was.

JAMES i:24

SOMETIMES when a man's memory lapses like that, and he forgets, it's a pitiful and disastrous thing. The story is told of a blinded, shell-shocked veteran of the last war, that during a convention of the American Legion he stumbled to the platform, and in the dead silence which fell at the very sight of him asked this one question: "Can anybody tell me who I am?" James presents us here with just such an un-named person. We know something about the poor fellow in this case. Not much perhaps, but something. He's a hearer of the Word. He's the kind of individual who's quite willing to listen to a sermon now and then, no doubt even reads the Bible occasionally, and once in a while goes so far as to attend a few lectures on religion. But he doesn't really act on any of it. He isn't a doer. It all rolls off, as we say, like water from a duck's back. Though the description here I suppose is more fitting. Such a one, says James, is like a man who gives a hasty glance at himself in the mirror and then forgets all about it. That quick survey of his isn't in any sense a constructive process. He doesn't stand there a bit and fix things up so that he will appear at his best. He throws in one peep for habit's sake, and either because he's satisfied with what he sees, or because it's hopeless anyhow, he turns away and dismisses the whole business. He beholdeth himself, and goeth his way, and straightway forgetteth what manner of man he was. But it won't be long—we are sure of this—until he's wanting to know. That's the tragedy of it. We've got to find out about ourselves, before we can set about living! Can anybody here tell me who I am?

Now I suggest that we stop our motion-picture just at this point and make a "still" out of it. He beholdeth himself. We'll take any man you choose and watch him staring at his own countenance reflected there above his dressing-table before breakfast. I wonder how many of us realize that it's a dilemma he's facing. He's caught on the horns of an "either—or." He is confronted with a choice.

He isn't exactly what meets the eye. I hope to show you that in a moment. He's either less or he's more. During the day, in a number of practical ways, he will have to make up his mind which it is. He's either going to sink, and turn out after all a little less than human, or he's going to rise and turn out a little more. He isn't even going to be rational. You follow him. He'll pride himself on being so, but it won't happen. He's either going to fall below the level of reason and live on his instincts, or he's going to struggle above the level of reason and with powers greater than his own live on his foolish, godlike dreams! By lunch-time he won't be just a man. You may count on it. He'll be a man minus something, or he'll be a man plus something. Between the two he will be waging the war which we call life!

And that of course is precisely the dilemma in which the whole world finds itself today. Here is why it's so appallingly restless and so transparently bewildered. Humanity hasn't decided once and for all whether it's plus or minus. Let's look into this a little more closely. I think we are pretty well persuaded, if we are sensible people, and remember a little history, that we aren't exactly equal to ourselves. The Greeks and Romans, to go back no farther, thought they were. They built up a civilization grounded on the conception of man as man, no more, no less, able to supply his own needs and to fight his own battles. The Greeks went in heavily for cultivating his mind. Looking back now we idealize most of the story, and call it the fair record of a golden age. But if you want to know what was really going on, take the word of one who lived a good deal closer to it than you do. Aristophanes puts the upshot of Greek culture very succinctly: Whirl is king, having driven out Zeus. After a while what happened to Greece doesn't make pleasant reading. Whereupon Rome came, with her ambitious program for the redemption of human life by law and order. Juvenal tells us about the filthy upshot of that. No—trying to deal with the human spirit merely on the level of its own humanity has never proved a startling success! Rousseau, in eighteenth-century France, was all for making one more attempt. You may read for yourself how it fell through. At the end, dissolved in tears over the death of his dog, he sent his five illegitimate children to a foundling asylum without a tremor! It's what always comes of adding a few fickle emotions to a fickle intellect that has no stability or support in either tradition or insight. You can't look backwards and downwards and enjoy long "the honor that belongs only to those who look forward and up." Somehow man never does exactly equal man! Let's remember that first.

And this second: that when man as now stands ready to call himself less, he's in for an even more prompt revenge than life has taken on his somewhat prouder past. At the moment he seems to be scared out of his wits lest anybody for instance think him an immortal soul. That would be too mediæval entirely! The world some five hundred years ago, you remember, was so confoundedly sure of being immortal that it didn't take time to be decent. For after all, what did it matter, with Eternity just around the corner? Not Prosperity, mind you—Eternity! You could burn a chap down here, if you had an idea that before things got too hot he might change his mind about something that would help him along up yonder! And even if he didn't change his mind, you had done no more than to light the flames of hell for him a bit ahead of time! I think you will find that most of man's inhumanity to man, from the year one to the Reformation, was rooted in a faith that tried to spend all its working hours in heaven, and left only its leisure for the earth. That's why we've reversed things with such enthusiasm and such violence. We've thrown out the baby with the bath. Immortality is too much for us. We choose to labour on the earth and aren't even sure that's worth while, devoting our leisure time to anything that happens to come along. Living is busier; but it doesn't mean so much! And the subtraction goes merrily on.

It's amazing, I tell you, this insistence with which everything that makes our world what it is keeps battering on our doors and shouting at us that we may be human indeed, but we've got a devastating minus sign in front of us. Mr. Stalin's State does it, and Mr. Hitler's, and Mr. Mussolini's—assuring folk that they are nothing but the minions of something called nationalism, ordering them about collectively in platoons. That's one aspect at least of every dictatorship. And Science does it, such Science at any rate as has become popular in the world; with its definition of life as a sort of breaking out on the skin of a measley planet, and its proud refusal to accept any moral responsibility for the use which men make of its discoveries: they can blast themselves into Dante's Inferno if they like. There's no Science of Man that cares anything about it! And all the while the Business Average tugs at you from morning to night to make you less than a human soul. The fuller life of which mankind is capable, and for which his heart yearns, isn't being forbidden by any statute: it's being rendered next door to impossible by the ceaseless demands of an ever-enlarging economic tyranny. You men who go down town every day are pitting your strength against appalling odds. You dare not be what those odds will make of you if they can! Should you let them catch you off your guard, you'll be less than men, more concerned with markets than you are with human needs. For God's sake go down there and do your best to lift this burden of things from human shoulders! I only warn you it's a heavy weight.

Little wonder then that civilization once more has grown powerless! Here is nearly the sum total of modern life: Business, and Science, and the State. Say what you please, here are the average citizen's loyalties. Unless he stands himself sturdily in their face they become his ultimate gods, on whose altars he kindles the tiny flame of his daily sacrifice. And there is a marked tendency among them all to agree in this, that what matters about man is the less than human! So that none of it really gets us anywhere. It renews no man's courage, beyond teaching him to whistle in the dark. It buys back no childhood prayers. "Beneath the crackling brilliance of our success"—so writes another, a keen observer of American life—"there lives a pathetic wistfulness. The treasure chest of the world has become a box of vanities. Its defences are a matchwood wall when sorrow comes in like a flood. The human soul, like a pilgrim of old bound for the Holy Land, takes its staff and goes, not in anger or contempt, rather in bewilderment and in discontent with itself, oppressed by a shallow breathing and a sultry air!" —"Can anybody here tell me who I am?" A man isn't equal to himself; and God knows it's bitter being less!

There's just one possibility left. It's this doctrine that as he stands there in front of his glass he's a man plus. The very things that make him a man make it necessary for him to be more. Memory makes him a man. It helps to separate him from the brute creation. And regret, and hope, and anticipation, and the substance of things not seen. All these make him a man. And they compel him to be more. They make him a misfit in this world of tangible reality, like a square peg in a round hole. They see to it that he's miserable, until he reaches out his hand and lays hold on God. They tease him and prod him and torment him and haunt him. The one thing they won't do is to leave him alone! So that the people who run from religion are like people running from hunger: the farther they run the hungrier they get! It may be that our educators are coming now to understand that. Dr. Hutchins of Chicago not long ago elaborated in a book his "new" theory of education. He doesn't want to centre it any longer about the pupil, as no more than pupil. We've been doing that for the last decade. You'd be interested to read his devastating criticism of our method. He wants to centre education around something given, some body of inescapable, stubborn, historic truth. He wants to centre it about God and the "goods of the soul." He remembers that there are something like two billion human beings in the world who aren't going to be content with anything we have been trying to teach them about themselves. They are going to leap beyond our poor assessments, and yearn, and believe, and throw in their lives, and write poetry, and set sail on perilous journeys. Walt Whitman can have his picture of a cow knee-deep in clover chewing her cud as his ideal of peace; but if he had ever achieved it he wouldn't have been Walt Whitman: he would have been a cow! The foxes have holes—Jesus put it that way—and the birds of the air have nests; but the Son of Man —and we lose the force of this unless we understand that Jesus meant not only his own but all the restless souls of God's creation! —the Son of Man hath not where to lay his head. He's forever bound to be more than he is! The winged bulls on the ancient walls of Assyria—you see reproductions of them in the museum—bear witness to that in us which, though akin to the beast, is nevertheless somehow obedient to "the heavenly vision of its own eternal dissatisfaction," and is poised momentarily for flight, "flapping and travelling in the winds of mortality."

So is religion—even in a measure false religion—never without its discoveries. The astronomers of Ptolemy's day were all wrong about the solar system; but they prophesied eclipses accurately! Columbus made use of a false hypothesis, and a route abandoned by modern navigation; but he discovered America! Religion is the only urge in our present world that's on the right track, childish and deluded as some of it is. In Christ it comes to you and lays a price on your head. What shall it profit a man if he gain the whole world—let's make it more specific: if he gain whatever it is that you're after, this side of God—and lose his own soul? It whispers to you of one who is strangely like you, and though ineffably great and holy yet stoops to pass beneath your portals. It leaves a cross on a dark hill to turn your spirit free, and sets your feet, with a steadiness beyond their own, on a road that has no ending. A man is a man plus, or he's nothing! That way, and that way only does he matter! "When I think," said another to me a few days ago, "of all the myriads that have been, and the myriads still to be, this notion that it makes any difference what I am seems silly. Why should I care?" For no reason, save for this: that since Christ there is more surely than ever something in the world that keeps taking off its hat in your presence, and ringing in your ears the sound of an ancient voice which says continually, Son of Man, stand upon thy feet, and I will speak to thee. You can't prove that the burden of this unending hue and cry it raises at the heels of every human soul is true. But I mean to live all my days as if it were!

I mean to see if in His company I can't still learn to gulp down a few insults instead of spewing them back. If I can't still learn to value my responsibilities in this world more than I value my rights in it. If I can't learn to go an added mile or two instead of wearily, so wearily, trudging the one that necessity demands. If I can't love a little where love doesn't pay, and suffer a little with patience for doing well. Oh, I shall blaze out angrily time and again, and lose my grip. I know. But I shall tell you then that I am not quite myself. And that will be right, quite right! Tomorrow maybe—or even yet today—I shall be up again and reaching! Because, you see, I think I am more than meets the eye!

A man beholding his natural face in the glass: he beholdeth himself, and goeth his way, and straightway forgetteth what manner of man he was. But it's never long until he wants to know! That's the tragedy of it. "Can anybody here tell me who I am?"

WHAT DO PEOPLE SAY ABOUT YOU?

*. . . as deceivers, and yet true; as unknown, and yet
well known; as dying, and behold, we live; as chastened, and not killed; as sorrowful, yet alway rejoicing; as poor, yet making many rich; as having nothing,
and yet possessing all things.*

II CORINTHIANS vi:8-10

IN THE sixth chapter of his second letter to the Corinthians
from the eighth to the tenth verses, Paul recounts the evil rumors
his enemies have been spreading about him, and balances them
with the facts: As a deceiver, he writes, and yet true: they called
him double-faced, you see, and he said he wasn't! As unknown,
and yet well known: they said he was a nobody, and he pointed
out how widely his reputation had run in the world! As dying,
as chastened—they kept whispering that his days were numbered,
and he was suffering the afflictions of the wicked: he kept remind-
ing the public of his deliverance—and behold, I live! They taunted
him with the solemn griefs he had had, and with his poverty—
sorrowful, they said, poor, and having nothing: he hurled back
in their teeth the joy that no man had taken from him, and the
wealth he had brought to a thousand lives—yet always rejoicing,
making many rich, possessing all things! It was a deliberate campaign carried on to undermine his influence; and he went about
calmly matching the slander with reality!

Here is something important enough, it seems to me, and near
enough to certain areas of our own experience, to merit some
study. Sooner or later, if you and I are to lead normally healthy
lives, we have to come to grips with this matter of the esteem or
disesteem in which we are held. It isn't for nothing that Kipling
devotes the first stanza of his poem to it:

> If you can keep your head when all about you
> Are losing theirs and blaming it on you;—
> If you can trust yourself when all men doubt you,
> But make allowance for their doubting, too:
> If you can wait and not be tired by waiting,
> Or being lied about, don't deal in lies—

> Or being hated, don't give way to hating,
> And yet don't look too good, nor talk too wise.

You may think you can shrug your shoulders and throw off what people say as being of no moment; but you can't. There is that inside of you that craves approval and shrinks from every man's poor opinion; and the craving and the shrinking do things to you! Somebody pays you a compliment, and you walk on air; somebody else doesn't, and you can't sleep that night! A few mouthfuls of praise may turn a man into an insufferable snob; and an afternoon's worth of buzzing gossip may flatten him out into a self-conscious worm with a crooked disposition! Unless somehow we learn to maintain our poise, as Paul did, between the two!

Let's begin with this: that of all the factors which go to determine your place in the world, what people say about you is the least significant. It does have its bearing, of course. Make no mistake about that. A man disregards it at his own peril. The weight of social disapproval is an awful thing when it gets into the scales against you. It can throw you out of any position you happen to occupy. It can hamstring a President, which seems to be Democracy's favorite pastime. It can ruin an artist, hang an innocent victim of circumstance, unfrock a minister, or wreck a home. That's why this business of bandying about careless estimates and idle verdicts with regard to Mr. A's abilities or Mrs. B's motives is so appallingly serious. It all helps to limit the sphere and narrow the horizons of somebody's life.

However, I am not minded to disprove my own case! In spite of the sobering evidence to the contrary which anybody can marshal, I still submit that what's being said about you matters least. Because, first of all, half of it isn't being said! It's queer how readily some of us come to believe that we are the topic of conversation in thirteen homes and on seven street corners! Someone looked our way once, or there was a strange lull in the middle of the room as we made our entrance! No question about it: we understand intuitively what they were doing! Every other subject from the Milky Way to the composition of electrons had been laid aside with dignity that attention might be focussed on us! And slowly the flush comes up from behind our ears! If the truth were known, they were doubtless agitating the unsurpassed advantages of the latest thing

in diets! Some such private and stealthy notion of our own importance, of the interest we arouse, and the figure we cut, lies at the
bottom of most of our sensitiveness.

More than that: when we've eliminated the half that isn't being
said, we ought to take a little comfort from the reflection that what
is being said is being said out of ignorance! Most of it, certainly.
There is hardly a word spoken about anybody that doesn't have
back of it some kind of prejudice, the bias of either friendship or
enmity, of love or hate or indifference. Frankly, people have nothing else to talk out of when they talk about one another! It's
clear enough that they haven't knowledge. They can't have. By
the sheer force of necessity, when the conversation veers over into
the realm of personalities, knowledge is left behind. Nobody has
any knowledge about anybody else! Impressions, attitudes, guesses,
must take the place of facts. That should make us more than a
little careful of the things we say, and it ought to be a sort of
solace to us when we hear that we in our turn have been up for
discussion! I commend it to you. Just to withdraw from good report
and evil report alike into that more or less bewildering mass of
first-hand information you have about yourself, which no other
soul on earth can ever really get at. When your public, be it great
or small, begins extolling your virtues, step inside and look around:
you'll be sure they should never have gone so far! And when they
start censuring your faults—well, in all likelihood, you will become
quietly aware in your retreat that they should have gone a good
deal farther! It's what Paul is doing here: he's stepping inside.
And honestly, he reports in his case, it isn't as bad as some would
have you think!

A man's estimate of himself, fairly arrived at and deliberately
pronounced—that's what matters. By the side of it, what others
say simply isn't worth worrying about! It's only when you take
home something they've said and entertain it, give it the keys
of the house, a little hesitantly at first, soon with more abandon,
until finally it has the run of the place—it's only then that what
these others say begins to take on real and vital significance; when
you start showing it the deference of your own belief! Writes Professor Hocking, "There is a deep tendency in human nature to
become like that which we imagine ourselves to be." You may call
me what names you please, from a genius to a fool, from a son

of God to a child of Satan—and none of it need have much power over me. But let me call myself these things, and grow accustomed to the thought; let me go habitually puffing myself up or running myself down—and bit by bit the very stature of my soul will respond to the constant suggestion! The same kind of subtle change comes over the men and women who keep calling themselves perplexed, agnostic, unbelievers; no faith can stand against such steady insistence. We may not always be what we say; but what we say, sooner or later that we are! It isn't the world's appraisal of you that should be occupying the place of chief concern in your life— it's your appraisal of yourself!

Let's suppose, then, that you have come with soberness to make out your report. It isn't easy. You would hardly suppose it a task for kindergartners, this that the Greeks called the very secret of life itself, and embalmed forever, like the riddle of death, in those two words, "Know thyself!" Surely it's difficult; but it isn't altogether impossible.

The first thing you have to avoid is all that over-rating of oneself which characterizes one half of our modern approach to this conundrum of existence. Christian people avoid it by pulling themselves up in the knowledge of God. I don't know how the others can ever manage without that, or escape the inevitable results of their own blind arrogance. When I was younger I was very impatient of the hymns in our book of worship which talked about men as though they were worms. I still flinch softly to myself when I sing them. But I know better with the years what the authors meant! You can't grow older before the face of this Christ without sinking, sinking, sinking in your own esteem. All your poor goodness has to crawl into his presence if it wants to get there, not like a whipped cur, or because he wants it so; but that's the way it feels, knowing its helplessness, never feigning, nor whining, nor fawning on majesty, nor excusing itself—just seeing in Jesus' eyes the daily beauty that makes it ugly!

Oh, our mood's against it, I know: we have a Humanism that wants us to stand up and look God in the face, if there is a God; we have certain youth groups that go about diligently counting up their good deeds per day; we have a thousand unhappy folk who won't be their age or do their job, because they think they're younger than they are, or abler than they are. But come and tell this God you meet in Jesus Christ how highly you think of yourself. Lord it about in front of his altar awhile; walk around through the Sermon on the Mount; pose with your virtues in Gethsemane and on Calvary. God pity you and me for the blasphemy of our daily swagger in this world of his with the blood on it! Have we never really seen ourselves?

To avoid over-rating oneself. And then to avoid under-rating oneself and slipping out by way of a sneer—"Who am I? I don't amount to anything!" Which is the other half of our modern mood. There isn't any book on earth that makes you feel more bankrupt than the Bible makes you feel; and there isn't any book on earth that smiles so, and covers you over with its hand, and sets you down by the grace of God above the stars, among angels and archangels. There's the eternal paradox of the Christian faith. It begins down here with Luther, "a lost and condemned creature," then lifts on the wings of the morning, "that I might be his, live under him in his kingdom, and serve him in everlasting righteousness, innocence, and blessedness!" It won't let you sneak away out of your inheritance and your destiny. It brings forth the best robe and puts it on you, and shoes on your feet, and a ring on your finger! On Monday they tell you you can't believe it because it does our sufficient and lofty selves the indignity of sin. On Tuesday they tell you you can't believe it because it does our brief lives on this distant planet all the honors of eternity. Why don't they make up their minds? It does us both! It reckons us poor and without any shelter of our own before God; and then it turns right around and catches its breath at what we are in Christ Jesus! I could never understand why a generation like ours, that wants to dream for itself great dreams in this little place, should dodge it so! You'll not dream as high as it dreams—until it catches a glimpse of what shall be, and stammers with awe, "It doth not yet appear. . . ."

And so—will you step inside this mystery of you and look around? What others say—does it matter? One can always get over it—with the facts and God!

WHAT ARE YOU SAYING TO YOURSELF?

When he came to himself, he said . . .

IF THE story of the prodigal son had been written in dramatic form, the first act would have shown you something of his unruly and restless youth, slamming the door behind it at last and setting out for pleasant scenes. The second would have introduced you to the boisterous hilarity, the sumptuous extravagance, the quick decline to sordid hovels, until nothing was left but a lean, ragged keeper of other men's swine. Whereupon one day he undertook to drop a word in his own ear: "When he came to himself, he said . . ." He took hold of the lapel of his coat, and walked away from everybody's hearing to have it out. The result was the rising of a curtain—act number three—on a long road, with home at the end, and a father's kiss. And all because that morning back there by the pig-sty he had talked it over with himself—so sensibly!

You see therefore that the practice has the most amazing possibilities, when a man indulges in it purposefully, with some intelligence. And all of us, I suppose, do indulge in it at one time or another. Of course the textbooks have a name for it, as they have for everything—creating by this simple device the illusion of knowledge: they call it auto-suggestion, and recommend for instance that on some sleepless night we should slowly rotate from right to left, pausing long enough after every movement to say "I can sleep in any position." Personally I think it's a much more dignified business, this: it's a human soul issuing its declaration of independence; it's a tamer of wild beasts, with his voice and his whip; it's a sort of Ben Hur gathering the reins in his hands: "When he came to himself, he said . . ." In any case the conversation is almost unbelievably important. Because when a man starts talking to himself he always listens, you may be sure of it. And he doesn't look around for a grain of salt either! This is a straight tip, and he swallows it whole!

And so I'm going to suggest an experiment. All language, like life itself, has three tenses: past, present and future. I propose carrying on some brief discourse with ourselves in each, just to see if we can learn to say the right things. To begin with, whenever we are on the subject, let's be sure to give ourselves very considered and accurate estimates of the past, instead of sentimental exaggeration and distortion. Too much romancing on the theme of "auld lang syne" is distinctly a liability, and not an asset.

Especially in matters of religion, I think, are we easily induced to take an overdose of it. We go off into ecstasies about some Garden of Eden where God once walked with men, and they heard his voice; or we remember the Age of Miracles, and sing songs, "I should like to have been with him then"—while anybody who knows anything knows that it's unspeakably better to be with him now! Then we come to the apostles, and build their poor human stuff up into gigantic figures, so unearthly and so huge as to put every one of their achievements out of reach once and for all; and we do this in the very teeth of the New Testament, which is always so painfully careful to keep them down on the level of their own often unbelieving and sometimes cowardly reality! And there is Paul, begging men not to think of him above that which they see him to be, or hear of him, wrestling with his thorn, exhorting that early Church, which so many of us have idealized as without spot or blemish, to have done with lying and stealing and all manner of uncleanness! And we complain that they had it on us!

Dr. Luccock of Yale has aptly called it "the haze of distance," which hangs low on the horizon and "envelops the past with an undiluted radiant glory which the past never had." And lest we suppose we are the first to suffer from it, he sets side by side two pictures of Israel on the march out of Egypt. Here is the poetry of a psalm: "He brought his people out with joy, his chosen with a song and shout,—not a weary man among them." And this is the fact, centuries before, written in the Book of Exodus: "And the whole congregation of the children of Israel murmured against Moses and against Aaron in the wilderness: and the children of Israel said unto them, 'Would that we had died by the hand of Jehovah in the land of Egypt, when we sat by the flesh pots, when we did eat bread to the full.'" "He brought His people out with joy." Read it with this: "And the people thirsted there for water; and murmured against Moses, and said, 'Wherefore hast thou brought us up out of Egypt, to kill us and our children and our cattle with thirst?'"

It will be a great day when we start telling ourselves the truth about these Titans of history, instead of weaving pretty romances about them! I haven't more than my share of patience with the modern school of professional "debunkers" who go about crashing every ideal they come across from Sir Galahad to Henry Ward Beecher; but they will have done us a service if they rid us of this fiction of super-men, and once more make us mindful of the common humanity we share with all those "who through faith subdued kingdoms, wrought righteousness, obtained promises, stopped the mouths of lions, escaped the edge of the sword, out of weakness were made strong."

"When he came to himself, he said . . ." Whatever else it was, it wasn't this, was it?—"Would that I were a Jacob of old, and could go back home as he did, to his father and his elder brother, with servants and camels and herds." After which no doubt he would have drawn a deep sigh, and stayed just where he was, murmuring "There were giants in those days!"

Let's leave that now, and get this conversation of ours over into the present. What sort of thing are you telling yourself about the current situation? You are exceedingly apt to believe it—don't forget that! In the prodigal's case it could hardly be called a situation: it was a pig-sty! He had made a bad mistake, and Life had turned on him with that grim, sardonic humor which sooner or later becomes familiar to people who make mistakes: of all occupations for a son of Abraham, a swine-keeper; and of all food, the husks they ate! It was pretty bad, no question about that! Here were the facts, and they were quite immediate. What to do with them?

Well just face them, first of all; and it's tremendously important to face them honestly. One of the most perilous things we do is to go on glossing over what we don't like about ourselves! We pin excuses on it, and polish it, until we can live with it comfortably. It doesn't consciously offend us any longer. And then one day just when we think we have got rid of it by decorating it and ignoring it, it leaps out at us and turns us into nervous wrecks! The wise ones at the hospital say it's what comes of repression: it's what comes of not telling ourselves the truth! Strange, but we are built in such a way that a man simply cannot fool himself successfully! He can't keep dodging the facts and stay well! That's why the apostle writes as he does: "If we confess our sins, God is faithful and just to forgive us our sins, and to cleanse us from all unrighteousness." It's good religion; and now, twenty centuries behind time, we have discovered that it's good psychology too! I would suggest that you get off alone in some window-seat and tell yourself what you won't let anyone else tell you. Start in at the beginning, and do it up thoroughly—where God can listen. Invite him to listen. If there is any charitable construction to be put on you, let him do it! Quit being polite to yourself, and have it all out!

"When he came to himself he said . . ." It wouldn't have been worth anything at all if he had gone on somewhat as follows: "I guess it isn't as bad as it looks; and besides, it's only temporary. If nobody I know comes this way I can probably cover it up, and get along all right. I must make the best of it."

Of course—and this needs emphasis—you don't want to make it worse than it is. The time Elijah ran off and hid in a cave—you remember how he complained that he was the only one left who had not bowed the knee to Baal? And God said there were seven thousand! The prophet was out in his estimate by some 6999! There are a number of things about your condition, I have no doubt, that are quite encouraging. One of them is that God's in it with you; and that isn't altogether negligible! Keeping pigs is bad enough; but it isn't the whole story when Christ is telling it! And the liabilities, however great they may be—you just watch it—aren't going to have it all their own way! There is something here besides swine, and a dirty renegade; there is a human soul, with its incalculable powers of recovery, and a Father, and somewhere yonder a home!

And so we have come away from both the past and the present to the future! I wish I could overhear your conversation with yourself on that point! That it's all going to be about the same as usual? Only you are just a little afraid it's apt to be worse? That there isn't much chance left of your being any different, or much happier than you are now? The best you can look forward to is monotony? That there are some things you can do, and some things you can't—and you have just about reached the limit?

I wonder if we could take a hint from David? Here he is in the forty-second Psalm, writing of the greatest tragedy in his whole life. His own son Absalom has raised a rebellion against him, and driven him out of Jerusalem. His tears keep saying to Him, day and night, Where is thy God? And all his memories are bitterness—of the days when he used to lead the multitude in the Temple, praising and chanting and holding high festival. Then, without any warning, he steps to one side and takes himself in hand. "Why art thou cast down, O my soul? And why art thou disquieted within me? Once the Eternal summoned for me his love by day, and in the night I sang of him. Send out thy light and faithfulness to bring me home, where thou dwellest! Cast down, my soul? Disquieted? I shall yet praise him, Who is the health of my countenance, and my God!" After that, runs the record, he arose, and came to Ma-ha-naim, where so many centuries before the angels of God had met Jacob. There is always that host to reckon on when a man lifts up his face and starts home! The very name of the place must have been for David like an answer to prayer! Having a heart to heart talk with yourself, and then—then stumbling that way in among the very tents of the Almighty!

"When he came to himself, he said . . ." Did it run this way?— "I'm here, and it looks as if I were here to stay. Going back will only make it worse. It's all over, and I'm done!" Whereupon he became very despondent. Strange fears beset him, and there was no psychiatrist in that country!

"When he came to himself, he said . . ." Pay attention now. This is the turning point. He's talking to himself. "How many hired servants of my father's have bread enough and to spare, and I perish with hunger!" No mincing of the facts! "I will arise and go to my father"—there's still a way out into the future, no excuses, frankly, fearlessly—"and will say unto him, Father, I have sinned against heaven, and before thee, and am no more worthy to be called thy son: make me as one of thy hired servants!" And he arose, and came to his father.

> To an open house in the evening
>   Home shall men come
> To an older place than Eden
>   And a taller town than Rome.

What are you saying to yourself?

Shall we leave it there now, with just this word of the psalmist to carry away?

"Blessed is the man whose strength is in thee, and in his heart—there are highways!"

ACCEPTING YOURSELF

But he answered and said, It is not meet to take the children's bread, and cast it to dogs. And she said, Truth, Lord: yet the dogs eat of the crumbs which fall from their master's table.

MATTHEW xv:26, 27

WHATEVER else that means, "It is not meet to take the children's bread, and cast it to dogs,"—it doesn't mean that Jesus was rude to her. Scholars who go about trying to explain it seem always to overlook the simple and, to me at least, conclusive fact that Jesus just wasn't that kind of person. He didn't hurt people's feelings when they came looking for help. We can at least give him credit, I think, for being a gentleman! What he said, therefore, you may be quite sure, did not fall as harshly on her ears as it falls on yours. If you read the Greek, into which somebody translated the Aramaic that Jesus spoke, you will find in the words themselves unmistakable indications of tenderness and affection. So that I am not at all concerned with what in English sounds like rather ordinary and boorish snobbishness. It wasn't. You may take that for granted. What concerns me is the fact that this heathen woman at once accepted the appraisal of this strange proverb and proceeded on it. "Truth, Lord: yet the dogs eat of the crumbs which fall from their master's table." She didn't go home and brood over it. It failed to induce one of our modern inferiority complexes. She didn't stop to argue that she was much better than this Jewish rabbi might suppose —which is what our present-day jargon would have called glibly enough a defense-mechanism. She wasn't the sort that had been eating her heart out in private because she couldn't be other than she was—a Syro-Phœnician and an outcast. She accepted herself at her face value, and persevered. "Truth, Lord: yet the dogs eat of the crumbs which fall from their master's table."

I wonder if you understand precisely what it means to accept yourself. It certainly doesn't mean being satisfied with what you are. She wasn't that. There is a way of accepting oneself that the man in the gutter knows all about. He has done so much of it that more often than not he isn't to be stirred any longer by anything beyond the gutter. To talk to him about "the pure in heart" is to arouse about as much enthusiasm as an earthworm feels when you dangle a butterfly before his eyes and want him to do his best! He has accepted himself, said "Thank you," and sat down! It isn't the kind of accepting I want to recommend at all. There is another kind, which rids the inside of you of an absolutely futile conflict, and doesn't kill desire. It makes desire effective. Let me illustrate it.

Here you have a child. You want her to be a pianist. At great pains you secure a good teacher, and at some expense. You bind her down to her practice. She dislikes it, and has no particular gift for it. So you change teachers and methods. There's no improvement. You bribe her, and cajole her, and ridicule her. You were a good pianist yourself, and you're determined she shall be. One day you realize you've done something to her in the process. You haven't made her a musician, but you've helped to make her a neurotic. She has got a fixed idea that something's wrong with her. The desires she had in art, or literature, you've frustrated. She has no sense of mastery in anything. And sometimes, because she can't win attention any other way, she gets sick headaches! We're very queer products of very queer forces, these selves of ours, and you ought to have accepted that child. What she needed was development, and you tried grafting. The only way you could have made her what you wanted was to have her very literally born again!

Perhaps it isn't necessary for me to say that you can bring about identically that same situation in yourself. You may very well go through life without ever really acknowledging the self that you are, dreaming of what might have been if only this or that hadn't entered in to complicate things. It began slowly to occur to you through the years that you weren't the genius you thought you'd be. The world was not as you had planned it. People didn't admire you as you hoped they would. You brushed against other shoulders stronger than yours. The figure you cut wasn't very distinguished. So you were inclined to be jealous and touchy. Without the knowledge you assumed its air. You battered the real self down and preferred appearances. Underneath all your thinking was your own condition. You set out from it and came back to it. And much that was unlovely got hold of you. And maybe you developed strange pains in your back—you didn't know why, but perhaps—it *has* happened—perhaps it was because most of us unconsciously argue that it's better to be something sick than to be little or nothing well! The psychologists call that conflict, and frustration—and they say we all suffer from it, more or less! I wonder if they are right? I wonder if you have ever accepted yourself? "He answered and said, It is not meet to take the children's bread, and cast it to dogs"; and she said, "Truth, Lord!" Would you ever, ever, ever in the world have said that? "Yet the dogs eat of the crumbs which fall from their master's table!"

Let's see then what there is about us that needs accepting. First of all, the place we occupy in life. It would seem that that might be comparatively easy here in America, where at least theoretically we proceed on the assumption that all men are equal. But we are able by one device or another to provide as many disastrous distinctions between people as there are castes in India. In the south it's your ancestor that counts; in the north, frequently enough, it's your pocketbook; and in the west, your achievement—with plenty of nondescript hangers-on everywhere trying to climb something called the social ladder. It's a rich soil for all sorts of personal tragedies. Proud mothers send their children to schools where they associate with others who are reputed to be just a notch above them, and then wonder what's happened to their discontented offspring! The absolute absurdity of it makes it pathetic—as if a fox terrier should lie awake o'nights trying to figure out some way of being received at the Airedale Club! It's just plain nonsense, as ninety-nine out of a hundred so-called "distinctions" between people always are. That's one kind of slavery you can help. And God only knows what release there would be in deliberately trampling it all under your feet! The only question that really makes a difference that matters is the question of whether or not life is any better for your living it. Let the Cabots, who speak only to the Lodges, and the Lodges who speak only to God—let them play with their blocks!

But it isn't so easy to accept your lot in the world if it's loneliness you are fighting, or homelessness, or childlessness. That's harder, and the devastations such things have wrought in human personality are simply beyond any kind of computing. From one end of life to the other stalks the spectre of being alone. Some of us gaze at it with wide eyes, and leap into marriages more tragic than any loneliness. Older people come up with it, and all their places seem desolate,

their purposes unfulfilled. And the answer to it all lies in one great
and final act of surrender, and the setting of one's face, if not toward
the good one *could* do, then toward the good one *can* do.

It's the mood of the soul that has learned to say Amen to God.
Sir Arthur Sullivan caught it and made music of it:

> Seated one day at the organ,
>   I was weary and ill at ease,
> And my fingers wandered idly
>   Over the noisy keys;
>
> I knew not what I was playing,
>   Or what I was dreaming then.
> But I struck a chord of music
>   Like the sound of a great Amen.
>
> It flooded the crimson twilight,
>   Like the close of an angel's psalm,
> And it lay on my fevered spirit,
>   With a touch of infinite calm.

"The sound of a great Amen." "Truth, Lord: yet the dogs eat of
the crumbs which fall from their master's table." "To give up pre-
tensions," writes William James, "is as blessed a relief as to get them
gratified." And that isn't only psychology; it's religion! There is a
way of accepting what you are, and instead of sitting down in it,
with all the unlovely results of self-pity, beginning with it, and
working out a gracious will that can outrun your own, and bring
you double the poor half you aimed at! There isn't anything in this
world you set your heart on so rich and full and complete as that
other which God can give, if down in your soul you discover the
chord you lost, and it's the "sound of a great Amen."

And so too with your equipment. I'm not suggesting resignation.
I'm saying that what every one of us needs is a mighty, resounding,
triumphant "Yes," deep somewhere at the very centre of our being,
to these selves that we are, with all their modest talents, their crip-
pling inabilities—and I say it boldly, with all their sin! "Yes"—
"Truth, Lord"—and out of life as at a stroke drop all the soured
ambitions that defeat themselves; hopes that have in-grown like

malignant, ulcerous things; visions once, stale, futile dreams now, pauperizing, invalidizing dreams—gone with that "Yes!" And it may be that for the first time in all your narrow days you are free to be yourself—in the forgiving, recruiting hands of God!

That's where I have been anxious to come out. For it's just at that point that psychology stops and religion comes fully into its own. The hands of God! I know what you'll say; you'll say, "There he goes off toward the mystic idealism into which Christianity always evaporates!" If there is anything mystic about getting this self of yours over into the hands of that God, if that isn't the most practical, straightforward bit of realism you can happen on under the sky, then you may as well burst this bubble of a Jesus-myth and have it over with: it's nothing but a little iridescence in a film of soft-soap around some tepid air. Go ask anybody who has said more than "Yes" to his own soul; ask the man who has said "Yes, but—" and with that splendid addition has laid down his own bleak loneliness, his bitter memories of sin and failure, laid them all down in those other hands: go ask him if there are any mysterious margins of peace and hope and strange fulfillment when God takes up your life.

This woman could have told you: "Truth, Lord: yet"—and into the brave poverty of that outcast soul strode the Creator, until he turned her "Amen" into a "Hallelujah!" Jacob could have told you, there by the Jabbok, wrestling with the angel, crippled Jacob: "I will not let thee go, except thou bless me"—limping on into the morning with a sweet, new grace of God in his soul! Paul could have told you, with his prayer, and his thorn, boasting of his weakness, that the power of Christ might rest upon him. Philip could have told you, and Andrew, that day they took a lad's five loaves and two small fishes, and learned twelve-baskets-full about these margins of God! Mysticism indeed! You go out yonder and make some trial of it! Dynamite, Paul called it, not mysticism—a little Jew, sick, stoned, beaten, and shipwrecked, in the hands of God!

That's your problem, accepting this that you are for the glory of that which he can make of you! I haven't any enthusiasm for anything that's this side of it. The wise ones of the earth talk about sublimation; which, as far as I can find out, is pulling yourself up by your bootstraps. They talk of self-analysis, and the process of realization. Let them talk. A plague on all their houses. I'd rather spend one half-hour in the presence of this clear-eyed Christ and let him strike my trammels off; until I stand free before him, ready for his will! He sees my worst. Let him speak. I'll hear him out. And then I shall say, "Truth, Lord: yet . . ." and I shall lay it all down at his feet. After that I'll be going about my business preparing for the miracle!

ON LIVING WITH YOURSELF

*And Jacob was left alone; and there wrestled a man
with him until the breaking of the day.*

GENESIS XXXII:24

HE COULDN'T sleep. He had to have it out with God and
with himself. He was coming back home after twenty years
to meet the brother he had tricked. All the old ghosts came stalking
around that night: the birthright he had bought, the whisperings
with his mother, the blessing he had stolen, the angry threat of Esau
against his life, the flight for a few days—days that had stretched
out from youth through marriage to middle age—until here he was,
on his long-delayed return, waiting by a little brook for the morrow,
and the man he had wronged, marching up out of the south. Present
after present had been sent on before to smooth down his brother's
resentment. Tonight he was alone with his memories and his fears.
He said later he had seen God face to face, and they had wrestled
there; and he was helpless, but wouldn't let go without a blessing.
And I suppose we may take his account of it: it's near enough our
own experience for us to understand.

Every man sooner or later has some such difficulty with himself
and God. There are times of crisis that result in what may well be
called a wrestling through sleepless nights; and other times when
the struggle dies down into little more than a daily nuisance. Some
people aren't able to put up with it long, and go to pieces. They
grow nervous and irritable and melancholy. They can choose their
own friends, and they can get away from their relatives: but they
have to live with themselves. And that's more or less of a problem
for all of us! There are so many selves we have to face when we put
out the light and pull up the cover: they are there in the morning,
too, all sitting around the breakfast table, and getting on the subway
with us, and leering at us across the desk at the office, playing two-
somes and foursomes around the golf links, squatting down under
the light at home in the evening; everywhere we go, the old self, and
the lonely self, and the sensitive self, and the anxious self: they're a
troublesome crowd, and we've got to live with them. By the side of

that job living with others is as simple as A B C. "Jacob was left alone; and there wrestled a man with him until the breaking of the day."

Take the old self. Let's start with him. He's variously called in the New Testament the old man, the old Adam. This fellow plays Mr. Hyde to your Dr. Jekyll. As a rule, he isn't such a pleasant customer. None of us cares to sit down and hold any long conversation with him. At least I hope not. If you feel differently about it, and what you have been doing with your life seems on the whole to be quite all right, and this other self which you have the habit of becoming now and then seems a rather decent sort after all, comparing favorably enough with the folk you know, why then I guess we'll have to skip your case as being one that's past cure, even by God himself! That's why Jesus had to go off and leave the Pharisees: because they used to stand up in the temple and say how thankful they were that they had done so well. They got along splendidly with their old selves. And so nobody could do anything for them. The man over there in the corner was having considerably more trouble, beating on his breast, without so much as lifting up his eyes toward heaven: "God be merciful to me, a sinner." He couldn't stomach himself any longer. Jacob couldn't either, on his knees as the sun went down, whispering in the dark: "I am not worthy of the least of all the mercies, and of all the truth, which thou hast shewed unto thy servant." And the prodigal, in the story that Jesus told, mumbling over and over to himself the words that kept time to his steps as he trudged along home: "Not worthy—to be called—thy son." It's the way you're bound to feel, if you have anything in you at all, when suddenly you come up with God; and then have to turn and face your own past, which has come sneaking into the room with you, and stands with its back against the door! And you can't get rid of it by reading a book or going to the pictures!

But the old self is merely the first of this motley crowd we have to live with. Second on my list is the lonely self. We have to wrestle with him, too. Bernard Iddings Bell in his book, "Beyond Agnosticism," says that the most dreaded threat life holds for us is not "pain or penury, or thwarted ambition, or even death. The ultimate bogie is loneliness."

"We may keep busy," he goes on, "and most of the time forget, but there come the devastating moments, unavoidable, when we

homesickness of the soul." "Wherever men have looked on their lone-liness in this light," writes another, "they have found it not a bogie but a blessing. Through loneliness they have laid hold of a power and a poise and a peace which God from old time has ever imparted to those who seek him in the solitary place of the Most High."

To the sensitive self he comes with the assurance of a dignity that lies not in what other folk say, but in the fellowship of One who stooped under a stable door to light a fire on the hearth of the world, and making as if to go away, forever lingers whispering, 'I have called you friends." No self that Christ makes great can carry long the wounds of "man's inhumanity to man"—save as Christ carried his wounds, the marks in his hands and feet of a love that could not be discouraged. It's something to lift your head when folk wrong you, drink one small draught of his cup, and be above the hurt, in the high tradition of that Galilean—of the blood royal of God!

And to the anxious self he enters with a peace that passes under-standing. I sat some days ago with two helpless women. I had brought them the communion of his body and blood. And as I turned to leave that great solitary house where they lived, bound in one of its rooms, a long sigh from the younger followed me out of the door; and the words of it were, "The peace of God, which passeth all understanding." I saw it on the face of a man who for months, unknown even to his wife, had been eating nothing but chocolate bars that their little daughter might have her oranges and milk. As he lay dying he began, with his paralyzed tongue, hum-ming "Onward, Christian Soldiers"; and the light of Eternity shone in his eyes.

Ah, my friends, let Christ in the room with these selves of yours. Let him have his way with them. Professor Overstreet in his book, "About Ourselves," tells of "a woman who dearly loved her hus-band and who declared that during those first days of married life something almost mystical happened to her. The rather sad, timid, turned-in self she had known for thirty years flew away. She almost waved to it, she said, so real was its departure, and a very joyous, confident self that was her husband's self and her own, a new self, came into being." That can happen with you, as Christ gathers up these selves and sets them traveling together until they are lost in him down the road that leads to the Kingdom and City of God.

Luther once put the secret of it in a sentence. "If any one should knock at the door of my heart and say, 'Who dwells here?' I should no more answer 'Martin Luther.' I should answer 'Jesus Christ.'" Out of the old self, the lonely self, the sensitive self, the anxious self, this new, emergent self, given to a great cause, in the freedom and with something of the stature of God!

ONE SOUL'S EPIC

A certain blind man sat by the way side, begging.
LUKE xviii:35

THIS is the story of what happened one day, very like other days, to a beggar who couldn't see. It happened because he listened, asked a question, made up his mind, stumbled forward against a score of restraining hands and voices that tried to push him back, and fell on his knees in the presence of a man from Nazareth. If that were the whole of it, I still think its lines would be piteous enough, its movement grand enough, for anybody to call it an epic. The sweep of it, were it no more than this solitary soul's adventure toward the light, would yet be stately and heroic. But that isn't all.

Back of it and through it and around it are vistas and shadows that seem to take shape as you read, until what sounded at first like a simple tale of private mercies assumes a scope and dimensions as broad and long as life itself! Suddenly we are aware that it isn't so much an incident: it's history we are watching! We aren't gazing down a narrow vista through a forest of trees into the distant past; we are letting our eyes range freely from end to end of a wide panorama that keeps unfolding itself through the ages. The tragic wistfulness of that blind beggar turns into the visionless waiting of the human soul, straining its ears to catch some meaning in the confused tumult of human life as it goes marching forever down the middle of the road; and here and there this man's, that man's heart goes wild, his lips come alive with the name of God, and he begins elbowing his way out of a world of sound and darkness into the miracle of sight!

"Hearing the multitude passing by, he asked what it meant." And they told him: Jesus of Nazareth! It would be strange indeed if back of the appearance and beneath the surface, that were the true significance of all this turmoil; if the noise that we call life really meant somehow the presence of God! Certain it is that humanity alone has never learned to live quietly and contentedly down here; from one generation to another it sends up the most appalling

73

clamor. There is something restful and still about nature in all her common moods; the placid grazing of sheep, the ripple of water, the call of birds. There is something dreadful and uneasy about man; building his cities toward the sky, ripping open the silence with the din of his hammers, pushing, striving, wrestling, turning earth and sea and air into a marketplace or a field of battle, as his humor is, mingling the shouts of youth with the despair of the weak and the whimpering cries of the fallen. "Hearing the multitude." I don't see how you can help hearing it if your ear is anywhere near the ground!

Only the meaning of it seems to escape us; especially now, that the hubbub has grown considerably louder than usual. Walter Lippmann heard it some years ago, just as it began rising to its new pitch of intensity, and wrote his book, "A Preface to Morals." Reinhold Niebuhr heard it with more discrimination, and wrote his book, "Reflections on the End of an Era." Apparently the old order of things is breaking up, and making a great deal of very special racket against the age-old stir and din of human life; but that's about all the popular mind is able to grasp. With regard to what's back of it, year in and year out, you'll find as little agreement as there would be in a crowd of blind beggars about the noises on the road! Some people will tell you with Mr. Dreiser, sadly enough, that taken by and large, there's nothing back of it. The whole thing is meaningless. There's no pattern anywhere, and no reason and no sense. Or else they shrug, with Mr. George Jean Nathan, and submit to you that it's none of their business anyhow! Economics, nationalism, the Soviet Republic, this eternal stir and hubbub—what difference does it make, as long as there's bread to eat, and such delightful patter to listen to as Mr. Woolcott's book so aptly named, "While Rome Burns"! "A blind man sat by the way side, begging; and hearing the multitude pass by, he asked what it meant."

I am suggesting to you that it still means God. "They told him, Jesus of Nazareth!" That something dreadful and uneasy about man is his soul, and the disturbing presence in it of one whose likeness it still bears for all its squirming!

Long ago there was a day when Ahab, the king, came striding out of his palace. Everything had gone wrong. A drought lay over the land. All he had known for years now had been the brazen sky, and the dust, and the murmuring of his people. He marched angrily

toward the gaunt figure of Elijah which somehow seemed to have
gathered itself together like an apparition out of the desert. "And it
came to pass, when Ahab saw Elijah, that Ahab said unto him, 'Art
thou he that troubleth Israel?'" There it is. That's not just history,
it's the whole of it: humanity plagued, pestered, harried; badgered
about by its own soul, heckled out of its comforts, chafed out of its
peace—with God in its face! A God who won't let it rest in a world
like this, as though there were no other; sends it out each day to try
its hand at fashioning that other, to grapple with lust and greed,
to build with gentleness and brotherhood; lets it lie down with "the
half of a broken hope for a pillow at night, that somehow the right
is the right, and the smooth shall bloom from the rough"; until one
eternal morning he wipes away all tears from its eyes, and stands
it on its feet in the only world where it really belongs! So at least
this book reads!

So at least an Abraham and a Moses, an Isaiah, a Jeremiah, a Paul
and a John, have flung back over their shoulders to us as the crowd
did to Bartimæus. You and I come plucking at their sleeves with our
questions. The noise yonder, we ask them, what is it? This uproar
that life keeps on making forever? And they shake themselves loose
from us, these men that see, with the only word they have ever had
time to utter: God!

If this then is to be our reading too of all the tumult of human
life: that it's God who is standing there in its face to unsettle it; if
that's to be our reading of this clamor within our own souls, why
then we've got to keep our beggar company! He scrambled up,
dropped his stick, his ragged cloak fell from his shoulders, and he
went stumbling out into the road, elbowing his way past all the
people that despised him, and called him back, and thought him
nothing, until he came where Jesus stood.

It means, I think, that you and I are not to let what we are—blind
surely, and with these paltry pennies we have wheedled out of
living: we are not to let what we are keep us from this Christ,
despising our own poverty, calling ourselves nothing. Writes another
with rare insight, "That I feed the hungry, that I forgive an insult,
that I love my enemy in the name of Christ—all these are undoubt-
edly great virtues. What I do unto the least of my brethren, that I do
unto him. But what if one day I should discover that the least among
them all, the poorest of all the beggars, the most impudent of all the

offenders, the very enemy himself—that these are within me; that I myself stand in need of the alms of my own kindness—what then? That I myself am the enemy who must be loved; what then? As a rule, the Christian's attitude is then reversed; and in that reversal he plays both himself and his God quite false; there is no longer then any question of love or long-suffering. Shall I say to this brother within me, 'Raca,' thou fool, and condemn and rage against myself? Shall I hide him from the world; refuse to admit ever having met this least among the lowly? Were it very God himself drawing near me in this poor and desperate form, shall I go about denying him a thousand times before a single cock can crow?" Blind Bartimæus! Never to mind the voices that call you nothing—a score of them in the crowd, a babel of them in your own soul—all chattering together. Of what earthly use are you, that God should wait your coming? Never to mind! Jesus stood, and commanded him to be brought! And all at once his lips were alive with the bravest prayer: "Jesus, Thou Son of David . . ." "What wilt thou?" "That I receive my sight!"

Is that what we want, too? Is there anything the human soul, sitting there by the side of the road, in its ears all the noises that are abroad and mean God—is there anything the human soul needs more poignantly than that? C. G. Jung, one of the world's most renowned psychologists, calls his recent book "Modern Man in Search of a Soul." The very title itself suggests that he reads life very much as another Book reads it, as I have tried to read it here. Man in Search of a Soul! And here is what he says toward the end: "Among all my patients in the second half of life—that is to say, over thirty-five—there has not been one whose problem in the last resort was not that of finding a religious outlook on life. It is safe to say that every one of them fell ill because he had lost it, and none of them has been really healed who did not regain it." Or listen to a letter which came to me not long ago from a distant friend: "My life is such a mess, and there seems no light, no hope anywhere, nor any way out. Are the things you say all true—really true; do they mean life and death to you personally? Believe me, there is nobody here who can help me; nobody to whom I care to talk. Is there anything anywhere to which one can hold, which means anything real and lasting? . . . Forgive me. Perhaps I should not write this; but do you understand?"

Sight! Is that it? Not so much that we mean, desperately, to be as we are; though there is enough of that: but that one day we lost our sight, and we want it back! To see as Jesus saw: the dignity of this self he has healed, and made to stand here a child of God; to see him, and get to my feet before his compassionate face; to see the way my life must run; and the world he loved, to love it, too; to see the chance I have; with this last word I heard in the dark lingering on forever, "Receive thy sight!" No philosophy that I know will ever do it for you—rearrange your dreams, and all the odd, blind notions you have had of this queer place, until they begin to make sense, with Christ there in the front of them, and your own soul constant at last down the ways of God!

Then, with the world there in your eyes, and the self he intended you to be, never to wish you were sightless again, back among the comfortable shadows where there was nothing to do but to sit and listen! There is a road for a man to travel when he sees, and a day's work to be done, and a death to overtake—not as an end that comes upon you, waiting yonder with your cup and your pennies; but like a king's ransom that by the grace of God you've earned! Never wanting to get off, or be spared anything—that's how this epic ends!

"ABOVE THE NOISE OF SELFISH STRIFE——"

HATH GOD INDEED SAID . . . ?

IN THE third chapter of the Book of Genesis is a familiar story. It's the story that's given us of Man's fall, the prelude of all his difficulties, that primeval occasion on which he first faced evil and chose it—with what disastrous and notorious sequel all of history has since had to deal! Maybe you think that's heading back pretty far, taking a wide detour to arrive at the present. We shall see. The drama is laid in a spacious garden. The most important bit of stage property, at the very centre of things, is a tree with forbidden fruit. There are Adam and Eve, by way of inhabitants. And a serpent. And there, within the brief compass of eleven verses, three towering questions raise themselves against the mind. I want you to consider them with me.

The first is put by the serpent to Eve. "Hath God indeed said, Ye shall not eat of every tree of the garden?" The population of Eden, numbering two, had had their instructions, and from headquarters. They knew what they were permitted to do, and they knew what stern caution had been set up squarely in the middle of the road. Here is the suggestion that maybe after all the instructions weren't authentic! "Is that so?" the devil would remark, looking at something else. "Did God really say that?" As if there were a catch in it, and only gullible people would take it literally. Which brings the whole scene up to date at one stride.

For there is no broader hint made in our day than this: that the ideas of right and wrong which we happen to cherish are not God-given at all; they are just the result of human experience. They have no divine sanction in any eternal order. "Hath God indeed said . . . ?" In fact, there is no such thing as an eternal order: there is only the way humanity has taught itself to act for its own good. We have no heaven-sent morals; we have habits, a pattern for conduct built up out of the wisdom of the past. If tomorrow we should find that over night covetousness, or theft, or adultery had somehow lost their disintegrating effect on human personality, we'd change our statute-books in a jiffy! And no superstitious reverence for God Almighty, or for "Jesus Christ His only Son our Lord," would stand in our way! For pity's sake, they tell us, let's remember that certain things are wrong because they are destructive of our highest welfare; other things are right, not because we have any word from above on the matter, but only because they are conducive in the long run to health and happiness.

Now that would be a satisfactory solution quite if it were not fundamentally and deeply false to the very experience it tries to explain. Unfortunately there seems to be something called sin in the world, and it's far more than wrong-doing: it's a missing of some mark. And the sense of guilt that goes with it is not just the sense of having offended against the welfare of the race. At the very heart and core of it is the sense of having offended against One in whose face is everlasting holiness. "Against thee," so runs the farthest cry of the human soul, "thee only have I sinned, and done this iniquity in Thy sight."

W. K. Clifford, the physicist and mathematician, calls that face on the horizons of life a fancy. "Its dim and shadowy outlines fade slowly before us," he writes; "and as the mist of that presence floats aside, we perceive with greater and greater clearness the shape of a yet grander and nobler figure, of him who made all gods and shall unmake them. From the dim dawn of history, and from the inmost depths of every soul, the face of our Father Man looks out upon us with the fire of eternal youth in his eyes and says, Before Jehovah was, I am!"—This same Clifford is reported to have hung once from the crossbar of a weather-cock on a Church tower—and by his toes! One may well believe it. Farther than these drunken gymnastics of his, comments another as he records the incident, man's intoxication with himself is not likely to go!

I say that the very experience of sin alone, and the mystery of it, should have sobered him: that Godward anguish which is the central conviction of every life that has come at last to grasp with terrible honesty the ultimate bearing of the wrong it has done. You can break the laws of Society or of Nature; but when you have acknowledged all your guilt before them, there is a surplus of guilt in the soul that lifts up its hands in supplication to the sky. And that isn't theory. It doesn't even seem to be superstition. We get rid of superstitions more easily! That too is experience, and you can't start putting together a philosophy of life by throwing it out of the window! In the whole terrific impact which sin makes upon one's self, there is more involved than some breach of custom, some disregard of man-made convention: God is involved, and somehow humanity has always known it, calling out with the prodigal while yet afar off and all out of breath with running, "Father, I have sinned against heaven, and in thy sight." That calls for as much interpretation as anything else I know, if you want to be true to the whole of human experience.

I suggest to you therefore that there is a moral order, and that it has its roots in something deeper than the wisdom of mankind, be that wisdom ever so wise: it has its roots in the will of God. If that isn't true, then where, in the midst of humanity's age-old inhumanity, did Amos come upon this: "Forasmuch as your treading is upon the poor, I despise your feast-days. Take away from me the noise of your songs, and let judgment run down like water." And where did Hosea hit upon this, among all the smoking altars of his people: "I desired mercy, not sacrifice." And wherever in a day of exile, when the wrath of the Eternal seemed so manifest that none could avoid it, did Jeremiah stumble upon this: "I have loved thee with an everlasting love." And Jesus of Nazareth—where did he happen upon that profundity of insight, that weird impressiveness and power which have combined to make his Sermon on the Mount, against all human custom everywhere, the noblest, fairest, truest word that was ever spoken to human hearts? "God hath indeed said . . ." I see nothing else for it.

Ours may be a troubled generation; but we can at least strike out this one absurdity: that we have been left to our own devices on the wrinkled skin of this pigmy planet, where nothing is wrong and nothing is right save as men condemn or approve it. If you think that the ethics of loving your enemy and blessing them that curse you can be settled by a vote, I don't! There is an inviolable will of God about your days, and it isn't subject to your revision! "Is it a dream?" muses Walt Whitman, and answers himself:

> Nay, the lack of it a dream,
> And failing it,
> Life's lore and wealth a dream,
> And all the world a dream!

So much we can begin with!

Well then, with that in our minds, let's come to these other questions. They belong together, and we shall try to hold them so. There is Someone in this story who is already away from home, with the dust of the road on him, and his voice is like a voice that men listened to once in Palestine. It was hardly louder than the sad murmur of leaves: God, walking in the garden in the cool of the day, whispering "Adam, Adam, where art thou?"

You will not find anywhere a more dramatic picture of the lost estate of the human soul: a man, with his life wrenched away from its fair, high promise, hiding himself from a voice that keeps sounding in his ears, and from those feet that follow, follow after! Perhaps there is some other word for our generation than this. Disillusioned maybe, or bewildered, or uncertain; but none of them seems so very much better than "lost." "Never was the landscape wilder," writes Mr. Lippmann, "or the signs fewer. Our fathers thought they knew their way from birth through death into Eternity: we are puzzled about day after tomorrow." Lost! And hiding!

Hiding behind three hundred pages of philosophy perhaps. Is that how things are with you? Or behind the latest book on psychology? You'll always rub shoulders there with the pick of uneasy lives desiring wistfully to be the most masterful of people. Or shall we say that you are all poised and ready to dash in among the devious ways of politics, where perhaps you can devise some plan that may not be right, but you want to see if somehow it may not turn out to be expedient? We wander about among the intricacies of economics. Possibly if everybody is provided with a higher standard of living, whatever that means. Or if labour can win for itself a few added privileges, without taking over any too embarrassing responsibilities. Until it's revealed to us that life can't be reduced to comfort, or the Kingdom of God made out of india-rubber! Or we dodge behind Science, that sacred cow of the man-in-the-street. I heard one of our multitudinous news-commentators talking the other day about the poor chap who was brought back recently from the Orient in the iron lung; and he closed his announcement with this brave assertion: "So does Science step into our world bringing its message of hope." Whereupon I suppose everybody leaned back and felt better! The tragedy of it is that we allow such facile nonsense to go unchallenged. Whether Science has brought us a message of hope or an abysm of despair rests with us and the use we make of it. Galileo fashioned

a telescope once; but that didn't keep the senators of Florence from
wagging their white beards, and plucking at their golden chains with
stiff old claws too feeble for the sword-hilt, and squeaking all at once

This glass will give us great advantages
In time of war!

God of love [writes Alfred Noyes, in "Watchers of the Sky"]
Even amidst their wonder at Thy world,
Dazed with new beauty, gifted with new powers,
These old men dreamed of blood![1]

Science doesn't bother much with motives, and unless there's something in this world that will, Science too lies under threat of death!

Yes, I think "lost" will do. Humanity, with all the world wrenched
away from its promise, hiding! And why? For no other reason than
this: that men have such a stubborn fondness for running off after
some poorer counsel than God's. See how it is in the story.

When at last Adam steps out from behind his worthless shelter,
and stands there naked and ashamed—then under the green trees
of Eden, swiftly upon the heels of the second question comes the
third: "Who told thee that thou wast naked?" Or to put it in
language more intelligible, "Where did you get this information
which has brought you such grim knowledge of yourself, and
wrought all the havoc?" "Who told thee?"

And what is there to say? What is there for us here to say? There
are Nietzsche and Karl Marx. We have got some of our information
from them. And there are Bertrand Russell, and H. G. Wells, and
Mr. John Dewey. We have got a great deal from them. And there
are Clarence Darrow and Henry Mencken and Sinclair Lewis. I wish
I could trace to all its sources this stream of our twentieth century
ideas about life and how to live it; then weigh them here in my
hand, many a goodly name among them, against the name of one
whom men called Jesus. With the apostle I shall still mildly protest
at the end, "I know whom I have believed."

There was a time within our life span, recently enough, when
Christianity itself looked as if it had half a mind to run off after
everybody who woke up on Friday morning with an idea. We heard
that most of the epistles and gospels would have to be adjusted to

[1] Frederick A. Stokes Co., 1922.

the modern view, to intellectual culture, and inevitable progress, and human judgments. Until there for a while the whole task of the Church seemed to be the task of accommodating all Christian thought and practice everywhere to everything but Christianity! That's why we have become so utterly impotent. We have done what Louis XV did when there was so much excitement about a few miracles alleged to have taken place in a certain cemetery in Paris. He locked the gates of the cemetery and hung a sign on them which read: By order of the king, God is hereby forbidden to work miracles in this place. It's a parable of our troubled age. We have been willing to do without the miracles. If 1938 should happen to need one, let it be by some other hand. God is out. We shall have nothing to do with Him.

Or will we? It may be that in these days to come we shall reach one or two conclusions for ourselves. And among them this: that Jesus Christ was right, and that by his side there is none else *so* right. We may, now that we have tried our "clatter of cults," decide that there is no other name. He stood against the Roman world. Perhaps he can stand against ours! It may be that we need not go on forever calling him a dreamer, complaining about how impractical he was, then tomorrow getting our hands back on something that's more practical, and never works! I know: we have nothing but a brief record of his words and deeds over a period of a hundred days or less. That's all that's left. You can't tell exactly what he would do now, if he were confronted with the confusion of our time—or exactly what he would say. And we may be grateful that we can't. Someone has pointed out that such knowledge might well prove to be the very death of the mind, and "the black pit of all our questing." But the voice is there, calling—calling by our failures and the ruin that's in the world. And the Spirit of God is there, forever in search of the human soul. And if not all his gracious words are left to us, there is at least his Word, the ineffable Word of God made flesh for our adventure! I wonder if we are not ready for it!

So do these three questions still raise themselves against the mind; and in them is to be read strangely enough the epic of all time. "Hath God indeed said . . . ?" Man, allowing himself to tamper with the eternal order, as if it were neither an order nor eternal; and then standing there ashamed among the trees, lost,—"Adam, Adam, where art thou?"—altogether at wits' end because he has run away after some poorer counsel than God's. I don't wonder that Peter, in his own critical hour of the long and bitter experiment called life, set up before the scattered Christians of Asia Minor this timeless challenge: "Sanctify the Lord God in your hearts." That said it all. Perhaps it may say to us all that needs saying. And remembering a day by the sea, recalling those quiet words, "Launch out into the deep," Peter faced a new world, with Jesus of Nazareth in its dangerous front!

MORE OR LESS

*And a very great multitude spread their garments in
the way; others cut down branches from the trees, and
strawed them in the way.*

MATTHEW xxi:8

THERE have been heroic figures that downtown New York
has welcomed in some such fashion as that, except that for
garments and branches we have used telephone directories and
ticker tape! But there has been the same abandon about it all, the
same refreshing recklessness as the spirit of man lets itself go, leaving all its neat and careful calculations at home in the ledger, snatch-
ing off its coat, throwing its hat in the air, and tossing on the road
any token of devotion it can get its hands on.

It was such a day in Jerusalem. People nodded happily to one
another there by the Bethany gate, and I have no doubt many an
old feud was forgotten. At last the Galilean was taking things under
his own management, God be praised! He was reaching for the
ancient sceptre. They jostled good-naturedly back and forth. A
group of children somewhere began to sing. The crowd took it up
with a roar. Somebody spread down his colored tunic; another ran
out with his, and a third: until there was a brilliant carpet of them,
with palm leaves rustling under foot. And then in a moment it
was over. The multitude poured past into the city like a tide, breaking in waves against the temple steps, its hosannas curling over and
pitching forward into the court where the money-changers sat, and
looked up suddenly startled. So silence came back to the streets.

Now the glory of the whole thing, it seems to me, lay precisely
in its lack of restraint. It looked as if everybody, with an impatient
gesture, were laying aside the prim tradition of being correct, and
moderate, and self-controlled. They meant to cut free, and tear
away, and be themselves once, with a generous shrug for all ac-
countants, and the prosaic folk who keep records, and read books
on etiquette! Here was a great soul, and they'd—they'd set the place
by the ears for him! You could tidy up and count the cost after
if that was your mood! More or less wouldn't do: it was utterly

88

now, top to bottom, altogether; and who's going to worry about what happens?

That brings me to something right away. It brings me to the peril of our careful lives. There is a sense, of course, in which a man has to watch his step, that near-sighted slogan of humanity in its jungle of machines. He has to take certain normal precautions about his budget, and his health, and the traffic, or this world he's trying to live in may smack him pretty completely out of the picture! A decent amount of care is clearly indicated in order to prevent your own unexpected absence tomorrow morning! But while thinking twice, and going ahead with prudence, and minding your P's and Q's, may possibly result in your living long, it can never on this earth bring you to live well! There is more than a touch of humor in the child's definition of an optimist as one who looks after the eyes, and a pessimist as one who looks after the feet! We are conscious of a fine and careless rapture, a sort of foolhardiness and knight-errantry, about living when it's at its best, like the freedom and form of a good driver, or the ease of an athlete, or the delicate balance of a skater—after the painful period is over! And it does seem that you and I so rarely achieve it. We want to take all our hurdles by crawling, and the only way to take them is by leaping!

We talk about being guided by reason; and nine times out of ten, if you analyze what we mean, you'll find that it simmers down to some brand of selfishness. Above all things our century desires to be reasonable. It wants to be reasonable about its religion, its love and its faith and its hope. It wants to be reasonable about its devotion to the cause of peace, in its quest for economic security, in its efforts at social justice. While the real trouble for the most part, to put it bluntly, is just that it's afraid of telling the truth, or starting to act on it with any enthusiasm! It's scared to death that somebody will call it a fanatic. It refuses, thank you, to be a fool for anything, no matter how desirable. And so it goes on currying fear and suspicion and war by brandishing around under everybody's nose its own mailed fist. It goes on encouraging revolution by shutting its eyes and supposing all things are as they were, still saying its prayers to a capitalist God, telling its beads to keep up the dividends. And we call it being reasonably safe, lest some unauthorized person upset the apple-cart, like a crazy prophet, and chuck everything for the sake of human brotherhood and disarming friendliness. I just wonder which of the two does make sense to you: our caution, or Christ's uncalculating gallantry!

When you get it over into your private life, this habit of keeping out of harm's way and feeling your ground makes an awesome mess out of things. It turns your Christianity, which ought to be a grand sweep of the spirit, into a laborious plodding along difficult paths. You are always figuring out how far you should go, and just where the trouble is likely to start. So you don't go anywhere. You try to maintain your balance by standing still, and smiling a kind of sickly smile when someone hurts your feelings, and holding on to as much self-control as you can muster. And that's the highest notion many of us have of what it means to be a Christian. I tell you right now, that's infinitely harder than it is to break loose in full course, heedless of the pain, running out upon life to change its spiteful temper with a forgiveness that keeps multiplying itself by leaps and bounds, seventy times seven! Religion is like riding a bicycle: the only safety there is lies in riding! Otherwise you can't even stay on. Momentum is the secret of poise. You'll spend all the days of your pilgrimage being upset, until you learn to fling yourself on such faith as you have, and instead of trying to put up with the wrongs that people do you, swing out to set them right! That isn't pious talk; it's common sense!

Most of this futile threshing about that we do in our attempt to be Christians "more or less" reminds one of a poor swimmer standing on the end of a diving-board, afraid to dive. Suddenly something tips him off center, and his arms begin to whirl like a pair of wind-mills in a frantic effort to get back on his feet; but all that comes of it is an unsightly splash and a horrible blubber. Which accounts, I dare say, for the major portion of our difficulties; and for all the hesitant Christianity that grows so tedious even to itself. We simply haven't the courage to plunge into what we know is right, though it were miles wide and fathoms deep. It's only now and then that these rare spirits come along, and far from being tipped off center, leap off, and cut cleanly into the cool green water! "A very great multitude spread their garments in the way; others cut down branches from the trees, and strawed them in the way."

So I come to the only other point I want to make if I can. I want to keep what we have already: that veering cautiously over to the

safe side of all the love and truth we know is not the way out of
disaster; it's rather the way into it. But I don't want to stop with
that. Let's go on and see what happens when a man actually does
throw that kind of caution pretty much to the winds.

Two things, I think: he suddenly discovers himself; and just as
suddenly discovers what it means to live, not long necessarily, but
by the grace of God, well! First he discovers himself.

Almost everybody is hounded and badgered about by the spectre
of a grander self than any he's ever known or laid his hands on.
In moments of confidence he will tell you that he has never in all
his life come anywhere near being what he is quite sure he should
be, not within striking distance of it. And he has tried. Make no
mistake about that. No use calling him a hypocrite. In the name
of Jesus, have a little sympathy! He may be a failure, but he isn't
a fraud. When you see him going to church it isn't a mask he's
wearing; it's a battle he's fighting. He's dreaming, just as you are,
and hoping, and praying, trying to turn into reality some glimpse
he has had of the best, and not getting on with it.

So there are times when he grows morose and difficult. He doesn't
make friends easily, and he begins to show his teeth and snap at
those who still try to hold fast. It's the only cover he has ever been
able to work out for the poor self he looks down on from the top
of his soul. He turns in on the lean thing, becomes increasingly
cautious, full of hesitations; starts reading books on how to develop
personality; he may even answer advertisements which promise to
make of him an author or an orator before he knows it!

And all the while the only thing he needs is a lesson in self-dis-
covery, so simple that the amazing thing is the few who ever seem
to try it! "He that loseth his life," is Christ's way of putting it; "he
that loseth his life for my sake, shall find it." There's no promise
for anybody who goes a quarter of the distance, or half, or nine-
tenths; losing doesn't mean tying a string around all you had and
fastening it to your belt before you let it go! Losing means that
you've thrown caution to the winds somewhere, about something.

There's no dearth of possibilities. It may be you can sink that
self of yours so deep in someone else today, tomorrow, that you
can forget it into a kind of splendor, and men coming to look for
you will find it hidden away like some cleansing, healing memory
in a score of other lives—as one finds Boswell in Johnson, or Eliza-

beth Barrett in Robert Browning. Or perhaps you can sink it deep in one of God's great plans for the future, the justice he's trying to set up among men, the poverty and dishonesty and crime he's trying to wipe out, the peace he's trying to bring on the earth.

It's tragic, the way some people stand around in a world like this and wonder what there is to do! One young person at Northfield, who had looked into the eyes of Christ, and had got her life out there in her hands ready to give it away, said to me that if she went back home and asked her minister for advice he'd probably want her to sink it in some Sunday school class! It isn't that we lack opportunities; it's that we sneer at them every time somebody shows them to us, and then march off with our eyes shut as though there were no others! Five minutes will reveal a dozen in the headlines of tomorrow morning's news! John the Baptist didn't have to cast about much to come upon one of God's causes, and he didn't have the printing press to help him; nor is it on record that he asked advice anywhere!

To choose anything that's greater than oneself and one's own safety, and instead of complaining about how little is being done nowadays; instead of criticizing what others are doing; instead of forever trying to spare yourself some added concern or a bit of trouble, to get into it with one's mind and study it; to get into it with one's heart and blaze about it; to get into it with one's will and live for it. You may keep tinkering and looking all you please; but you'll never find another road into the undiscovered country of your own soul! "He that loseth his life for my sake shall find it." There's one thing that happens when a man learns to throw our kind of caution to the winds!

And here's the other. He learns that the ultimate secret of the good life is not restraint; it isn't in the following of rules, or in obedience, or in loyalty; it isn't even in the daily imitation of Christ: the ultimate secret of the good life is in the freedom of this that I've been talking about, the freedom of a high and unbridled devotion.

Long ago that freedom was in God, when he threw away all the numbers men can count and scattered his limitless bounty across the sky and over the hills and in the fields, to make trees and stars and flowers; when he spread his mercy over the doomed city of Sodom ten times farther than Abraham had prayed, until it reached in and covered Lot, the one near decent soul that walked the streets. It pressed on through the years and poured itself out over a strange and rebellious people. There were whisperings of it on human tongues: "I have loved thee with an everlasting love; I have called thee by name; I gave Egypt for thy ransom, thou art mine." It came to dwell, like the unreckoned largess of the spring, in the heart of a Nazarene, getting itself said casually to a lone woman of Samaria. It overflowed into the lives of a few fishermen, who shook themselves free in it, as boats rise on the tide. They saw that life, with this Saviour of men, was not something to be hoarded; it was something to be flung recklessly away. They looked at him in utter amazement when he said that; but they soon saw that he meant it. He held out his own life for any one of them to take. He got Himself deliberately into their loneliness, stooped down under their burdens, ran away into their parched souls like a brook, knelt with the very gentleness of God to wash their feet, and at last in the ecstasy and grandeur of a yearning heart stretched out his arms on a cross to redeem them, and died with a prayer on his lips! That was life, free life, rich life, life as God intended it to be; and they hurried off into the hot sun, sure, quite sure, that every lavish hour a soul could spend would bloom forever!

It was the mood once more of that mad-cap crowd by the Bethany gate. Every one of the evangelists remembered it and set it down: "A very great multitude spread their garments in the way; others cut down branches from the trees, and strawed them in the way." Any token of devotion they could get their hands on would do!

I wonder if this generation of ours, after all, hasn't fallen a victim to the perils of a cautious life; with none of the full-hearted stateliness about it, the open-handed chivalry that one careless, happy day brought a throng of Galilean peasants to forget itself into immortality!

THE THIRD MILE

*Let us not be weary in well-doing: for in due season
we shall reap, if we faint not.*

GALATIANS vi:9

JESUS once pictured at a single stroke the spontaneity and abandon of the true Christian spirit: "If any man compel thee go a mile," he said—and I can fairly see him throw his arms wide—"If any man compel thee to go a mile, go with him twain." It is not easy for us to reconstruct the circumstances which rendered that gesture so absurdly generous, so unbelievably prodigal. America is a free country, and for better or for worse, compulsion has pretty well dropped out of our vocabulary. It was a stalwart word in Palestine, with the drive of a mailed fist behind it. It might meet you on your way down town tomorrow in the form of a Roman soldier, and jerking you by the arm say "See here, you gutter-rat, what's your hurry? Give me a hand with this knapsack of mine!" And you would not answer "I beg your pardon, but that would make me late at the office"; or "Excuse me, but I am trying to get to the matinee before the curtain rises." Not if Rome knew herself! You would chuck your business and your theatre and get under! Simon of Cyrene had to do it when they were driving a man with a cross toward Calvary. It was a pleasant way the tyrant had from over the seas!—galling, humiliating—the curse of God on her! And Jesus said, "If any man compel thee to go a mile, go with him twain!" And he said it to one of the proudest races that ever spat from an alley-way at the tread of conquering legions! There is something thrilling about the spirit that can lift its face out of a situation like that, and with a smile double its obedience! "Go with him twain." It is what we have come to think of and idealize as "the romance of the second mile."

But did you ever give any thought to the third? After the good impulse has very largely run off in sweat? When instead of your first flush of enthusiasm you are hot and out of breath; when in exchange for your generosity you have got tired legs and a pain in your back? What then?

I am taking it for granted that that experience is not wholly foreign to any of us, that or something like it. There is a glamour about all life and work and love when they swing up to their beginning, and the zest of their youth is on them. And then gradually the fine, upward sweep of it seems to level out. There is very little thrill about it now. The music falls into slower rhythm and minor keys. There are fewer bursts of poetry. The years turn prosaic and pedestrian, and there is only the dust on them, the dust of that endless procession of common days.

Yes, we are concerned with this. And so, I think, was Paul, if one may judge by what he wrote from his prison: "Let us not be weary in well-doing!" It is a road-warning for the man who has been a Christian about something until he is sick of it! He has turned the other cheek, he has thrown in his coat when they sued him for his shirt, he has loved his enemies, and blessed the people that cursed him. And the shine has worn off. And the trimmings fail to glitter as they used to. And "O Lord, how long?" becomes his favorite psalm. He did not calculate that the thing would keep up forever! "Two miles." That was an adventure. It was splendid! But three? "Listen!"—and he takes you by the lapel of your coat: "I signed up for an experiment; I did not sign up for a habit!" "But that is just what you have done," says Jesus, and strides on ahead of all our weary sevenfold forgiveness with his joyous "Seventy times seven." That second mile of ours was only a starter; three, four, five. It's all very well to climb mountains with your pulses tingling; but how about the prairie, plodding on and on; six, seven, eight! Grim going now, isn't it? And you clench your teeth; nine, ten, eleven! God! Where is the romance of that?

We must simply make up our minds whether we are going to fall victims to this mood or not. Sooner or later it overtakes everybody: but nobody has to lie down under it! The romance of the second mile has a way of giving place to the peril of the third; but you and I do not have to yield to its humour, we whose loads are heavier than we thought they would be, and the years long, and those places rubbed sore with the harness, and no light yet—until sometimes we wonder where the mercy of God has gone. There is such a thing as holding on! This much we know at any rate: that victories are fashioned in that third mile, not in the second! Sir Walter Scott tells us how true it was even of Napoleon, with

whom perhaps very few have associated "the courage of routine."
His was no vivid or startling bravery; only a great willingness to
go through with it, and on, and on, where "the lone and level sands
stretch far away." That place where the color fades and the light
goes out, you think it's a barren desert; and it's the still womb
of all the future, out of which shall come struggling into life every
laboured high fulfillment you are destined to lay your hands on.
It is in the dust of that same "endless succession of common days"
that triumphs are born! There is a book called "The Worst Journey in the World," written of that brave martyr to the quest for the
South Pole whose name too was Scott. In it is set down the story
of Gerard, the youngest of the party, on the endless trek homeward
across the unbroken ice. They were relying on him, the rest of
them; one more lost or crippled, and they would all leave their
bodies there. And his feet were frozen. On and on the rhythm of
his steps seemed to beat their message into his brain: "You have got
it in the neck, you have got it in the neck, you have got it in the
neck," with the crunching of the snow; when deep from the vast
silence of the white Southern waste a whisper grew like an answer
in his soul: "You have got it in the neck, you have got it in the
neck"; "Stick it! Stick it"—"You have got it in the neck." "Stick
it! Stick it! Stick it!" And they came through.

Grimness like that will always wear its medals somewhere, and
have its flags, and hear the shouting; but it is not the gospel. And
I am not content with it. It is not enough in itself to

> Give back the upward looking and the light,
> Rebuild . . . the music and the dream.

And that is what I covet for you; not a sort of resignation, with
its mind made up to "stick it," dull-eyed and dogged. That is not
what Paul means at all. Please get the full force of what he says.
"Let us not be weary in well-doing." It is more than a matter of
"keeping on," splendid as "keeping on" may be. It is freshness and
zest again, the tides of life flowing once more at the full; not weary,
no fag now. And I want you to remember what Paul has come
through, with that smile on his lips, and his eager gesture, and the
large, running hand with which he writes. His whole life has
been twisted away from its original purpose. Launching out on
his new course at thirty-five, for twenty years he has laboured in

the face of disappointment and persecution. Every step contested by Jews and Gentiles without, and Jewish-minded Christians within, he has pushed out the boundaries of this kingdom, almost single-handed and alone: Galatia, Asia Minor, Macedonia, Greece. And now word has come that the Galatians have fallen away into Judaism. Twenty years, and it looked as though all he had done might fall apart! And he is still marching, with his head up, ready to sing doxologies at every turn the road takes! "Not weary," not even weary! Only "the music and the dream!"

If you ask what it is that is holding him so, I think he will tell you. It is love, and there is a far-away look in his eyes: his love for a man who lived so cleanly, spoke so gently, died so gladly; and that man's love for him! You see, Jesus was an hourly reality to Paul, not someone he had heard about, but someone he knew, whose heart was very tender, whose hold was strong as God's! Every morning a voice, "Follow me"; and every evening a whisper, "Well done, friend; be of good cheer!" And you with your troubled hearts and slow feet talk of weariness! With Christ here? You cannot even manage to be refreshed by him? A love willing to be crucified, with forgiveness on its lips, holding out its arms; and you will not even rest in it? No song, no shout, no tears dashed away? God's love so futile as that? Galilean, with your yearning, your hands and your side, we are tired now, and all out of sorts. We have listened to your promises, and they do not stir us any more. There have been times when we have heard your footsteps with us, but we choose to be listless today and alone! Leave us, and let life have its way with us. That is our answer: we are spent; our answer to everything, from Bethlehem to Gethsemane; we are spent! And this man marching, five years, ten years, fifteen, twenty!

And in his heart a sense of the harvest; not his harvest, but God's! "Let us not be weary in well-doing: for in due season we shall reap, if we faint not." It could not be otherwise: the word of this Christ was pledged to it. Let it be slow; if God could wait, he could! Let them hound him down, and tear a year's work to pieces before his eyes: there was one whose will was good, and no man could say it nay. On and on, to Corinth. "In all these things we are more than conquerors!" Jerusalem. Rome. And there his triumphant soul sweeps out through his letters like an anthem: "I bow my knees unto the Father of our Lord Jesus Christ, that ye may comprehend the breadth, and length, and depth, and height, and know the love of Christ that passeth knowledge; who is able to do exceedingly abundantly above all that we ask or think . . . in every prayer of mine making request with joy. My God shall supply your need, who stood by me and strengthened me, and will preserve me unto his heavenly kingdom: to whom be glory forever and ever. Amen." Sit there now and think of his harvest, this fool for Christ's sake, this dreamer of dreams that God outstripped! And you—weary! You and I talking of our faith, and losing step the moment it's really tried; rarely patient except when life goes smoothly, fallen to wondering if God is in his heaven because life has turned rough? And this man—marching! "Let us not be weary; we shall reap!" Marching with the love of Christ upon him toward all that God intended! Visionary, is it? Well, I sat with a woman once as she came upon that will of Christ for her life, and I saw her stand up, and turn her face again to an old task, with the freshness of the dawn about her! "Not weary." No fag now! And I remember another, and the battle they fought for his life. Finally as he lay in the hospital at the end of the years, half his face destroyed by the slow disease no knife could stay, a friend came in and at the sight burst into tears. "Oh, no; don't do that!" came gallantly through the bandages; "my sword is still in my hand!" "Not weary . . . we shall reap!"

LIFE, LABOR, AND REWARD

*Why stand ye here all the day idle? They say unto him,
because no man hath hired us.*

MATTHEW xx:6, 7

THE afternoon sun was dipping down toward the sea; the
shadow on the dial neared five; and in the market-place at
Nazareth, little groups of men stood idly about. It seemed a heavy,
dismal sort of hour. But suddenly the whole square, as by common
consent, came to life. A brisk business-like figure had hurried in
from the street that ran away to the west. They made room for
him expectantly. And well they might. He was the largest single
employer of labor the village afforded—the owner of the vineyard,
which as everyone knew lay over there at the other end of town.
Four times already during the day he had come with his offer of
work. Surely it was too late now for them to hope. But with a
swift glance, for he was a man of action, he looked around the
circle. They shifted restlessly from one foot to the other. "Why stand
ye here all the day idle?" Fingering their caps, or whatever was
the equivalent, they told him why: there had been no market;
"No man hath hired us."

I can't tell you at all what Jesus was doing in the market-place
that day, but it seems quite certain he was there, and walked home
with the householder to see what the issue of this common, but
meaningful drama would be. At any rate, he used the story with
telling effect when Peter asked him, years later, what the wages of
discipleship were in the Kingdom of Heaven. You remember it—in
the twentieth chapter of Matthew—the workmen who went early
into the vineyard and pressed their careful bargain for a penny a
day, good wages; and those who went in late, without any bargaining—but got just as much. I think Peter saw the point—and I
hope he blushed! There are times when dickering isn't good business! I suggest to you then that we begin where Jesus began, with a
chapter on the Christian Philosophy of Life. We must, if we are
ever to get this business of living straightened out again.

The fundamental difficulty with our Western civilization is simply that it has never made up its mind as to what Life is all about! Some call it silly and grow cynical. To others it seems like a madhouse. One popular philosopher cries "What's it for?", and leaves it at that. There are very few prophetic notes anywhere as to its source, or its destination, or what it's supposed to be doing on the way. Nobody seems to know where he comes from, and nobody seems to know where he's going: you can't expect very much clarity as to why he's on the road! And so humanity has found refuge in a sort of hand-to-mouth philosophy. It has come to think of Life as a kind of glorified grab-bag, an emporium with long aisles of novelty-counters and "gents' furnishings," where almost anything may be had for a price. It sells the labor of its hands; it sells the best hours of every day; there are times when it sells its soul— for apartments, and balloon-tires, and electric refrigerators. And when you make so bold as to set some signal against its idiotic traffic, it turns on you and shouts, "Shall I not do what I please with my own?" It borrows the householders' language, and the householder here in the story is God! "Do what I will with my own!" Is that it? Have we taken at last to a blaspheming mimicry of God?

The fact of the matter is, and there is nothing quite so evident: Life isn't ours! We've done what we would with it, and the issue is what we wouldn't! Somehow, with all our air of proprietorship, it refuses to take its orders from us. If we do own it, something has gone wrong with the administration; that's certain! It has come to be absolutely and manifestly unmanageable.

God's text-book on economics starts out with the supposition that not only theoretically but very practically life belongs to him! Jesus calls it a vineyard, and says we are related to it by a very simple process: "Go"—and by a quite unmistakable promise: "Whatsoever is right, that shall ye receive." I wonder if it's possible for anybody to convince us that that's precisely the case? I wonder if we are tired yet of talking like God: "Shall I not do what I will with my own?" I wonder if America is tired of it, this solemn King Midas with asses' ears! One thing is sure: we've either got to quit it, or the noose is going to tighten! This world is not God's by human courtesy: it's his by eminent domain—and it seems to me he has been saying so pretty clearly of late. Maybe we'll use it differently when there dawns on us at last a decent conviction that it belongs to Someone Else! We don't misbehave so badly in other folk's houses—only in our own!

The second chapter of this story that reads so much like a text-book, I am going to call "The Christian Philosophy of Labor." You will have to remember I think that the first batch of men sent into the vineyard insisted on their contract: "When he had agreed with the laborers for a penny a day." All the others, the hour being late, decided to go in without any bargaining. And they came off best, you know. That's the point of the story. Peter got it, with his question about the wages of discipleship. He made no further inquiries on that score. It isn't primarily a question of what you can get out of life. If you have a dividend-complex, the Sermon on the Mount sounds like thin oatmeal! What seems to matter, in the mind of this strange Galilean, is the sort of investment you're making!

It may be we shall not like this so much. I still recall listening to an address which purported in all earnestness to lay down the average ideal of the average American: that every man should have a living wage; that every man should have his leisure; and that every man should have his share of the world's comfort. These things are important; and one may well be a passionate advocate for every feature of such a program as against the injustice of an economic order which would rob men of them. But it's another thing entirely for one to make a ruling passion of them. And seeing the multitudes, he went up into a mountain, and sat down and taught them saying, "Blessed are all the people who have a living wage. Blessed are they who are at leisure, and have their share of comfort!"—Because too many of us have minds like that, all up and down the economic scale, work seems popularly to be regarded as a curse, to be undergone merely for the sake of what it's able to produce! It's a word that startles many of the children in our modern schools. It's startling a number of folk who thought they could ride the Bull Market into clover! Work! What the sweat of a man's brow can do for God and the right, for justice and peace and decent human life! I submit that to you as the only philosophy in the world that will ever count!

Don't you wish sometimes that our billboards and magazines would quit advertising the things that don't matter, the stuff you can get if you have the price? What a desert it is, this balderdash held out to you as pay for your work! How would it be to advertise instead the contributions men and women could make: a great electric sign showing a teacher in the class-room, and a policeman on the street, and a doctor in his office, and a mother with her children—something that really matters? How would that be? Is this "getting" psychology of ours simply beyond the possibility of any change?

It's almost proverbial with us that Jesus, with his way of life, is visionary: it's the world that's practical. Well, for something that's practical our way of going at this business of living has yielded strange results of late! Christ seemed to think you could organize it around some other motive than personal gain, with every man for himself and poverty take the hindmost. We've been just as sure that nothing of the sort could ever be done. Who would work for anything else, we wanted to know—anything but what he could get? And there all the while to refute us was the fact that nobody who ever amounted to anything worked for that. No Milton, no Schubert, no Lincoln, no Pasteur, no Einstein!

What kind of contribution are you making to human life? That's what Christ wants to know. And perhaps it isn't so visionary after all! "A social system," writes Mr. Fairchild in Harper's, "that allows itself to be dominated by the profit motive is doomed to recurrent calamity and eventual catastrophe." Mind your investments. It doesn't sound so very impractical now. It may be that the dividends will take care of themselves!

And that I think brings us to the third chapter: the Christian Philosophy of Reward. Let's prick up our ears now and pay some attention to this story. I'm going to suggest to you that God's penny-a-day means happiness. That's the wage we all want, isn't it? And we have such odd notions about it. Most of us somehow seem to think it consists in becoming independent. It's positively appalling what a hold that has on us. We want to be independent of street-cars and have automobiles. We want to be independent of space and have radios. We want to be a little more independent of time and have airplanes. We want to be independent of coal and have oil-burners; of ice and have an electro-lux. And finally we want to be independent of work, and retire on our independent means. It's pathetic how wretched a man can be when he achieves all that shining independence!

God's idea of happiness is that it consists simply and solely in being useful to somebody. Not a bit of good setting out on a quest for it, Peter. You'll not make connections with it in youth by securing a good position and getting married, or in the forties by owning property, acquiring a reputation, and perhaps getting unmarried. That's the kind of pilgrimage humanity has been embarking on from time immemorial, and it's simply littered with failures from one end to the other. Somehow it seems that "go-getters" need not apply.

Nor folk who want to kick over the traces and do as they like, with fine freedom. Says Alexandra, a successful woman of the West in one of Willa Cather's novels, to Carl, a Wanderer in Eastern cities: "I'd rather have your freedom than my land." Carl shook his head mournfully. "You would be missed," he answered. "Off there in the cities there are thousands of rolling stones like me. We are all alike; we have no ties, we know nobody. When one of us dies, they scarcely know where to bury him. We live in the streets, in the theatres, looking about at hundreds of our own kind and shuddering. Freedom so often means that one isn't needed anywhere." No— getting out of the harness works no miracle.

The fact is, happiness is just the inevitable result of a certain kind of life. If you don't believe it, go about among your "kinship and acquaintance" and pick out the unhappy people, the frustrated people, and see how they spend their time. Then get hold of the radiant few—you'll know them by their faces and their bearing. I'll lay you a wager they've spent their time making themselves not free and independent but sympathetic and indispensable! Are you lonely? It is written of One that "he could not be hid"; and it's no secret. Folk needed him, and never yet have left him alone. The world knows to what doors it must build its roads! Sometimes it builds them even to bedsides where patience waits, and cheer. After all, happiness is a will-o'-the-wisp only to the man who pursues it: it settles down ever so gently like a homing-dove in the hands that each day give of their best however humble that best may be.

> There are scars in His hands and feet
> But a joy that will never depart;
> My hands are so smooth,—it's meet
> That the scars should be in my heart!

The thorns lie soft on His brow;
   In my soul they are poisoned with shame
That no one ever will now
   In gratitude murmur my name.

The wound still gapes in His side—
   And yet there is peace in His eyes!
For me, with the out-going tide
   Just a self—where memory cries!

Life, Labor, and Reward. It's strange that all the facts and figures should still be from Nazareth! Life a vineyard that's God's; Labor, the investment you make; and the Reward—happiness, a by-product along the way of a life Galilean and Christ-like. It's going to take some readjustments, I know. It's a queer philosophy. But the one that went to pieces in 1929 is queerer still!

ON CREATIVE LIVING

Be ye doers of the word, and not hearers only.

JAMES i:22

IN GREEK, the word for doers and the word for poets are identical. So that it matters very little how you translate what James says here. "Quit listening and do something" is all right; and it represents very well his impatience with people who keep listening to the gospel without ever putting very much of it into practice. Or you may say, "Come on up out of the audience and try your hand at being a poet yourself!" That would be all right too. The language would stand it. And somehow I like it better. Because if you ever mean to be the kind of doer of his words that Christ wants you to be, you have to be something of a poet! Just to go around prosaically and with great effort trying to act out the Sermon on the Mount won't work. You've got to put some imagination into it. You've got to come at living creatively, willing to face every "harsh bewilderment" it can bring, and out of the great "Yeas and Amens" of God, as out of words and letters one would write a ballad, fashion for yourself some new creation, each soul's different from the rest, but with the sign and seal of Christ upon it!

That's why I'm asking you to think here of the kind of living that's creative; and I want to begin by setting over against it, for purposes of contrast, the kind that isn't. Most of our normal human conduct can be divided into two great general, popular types.

The first is that often selfish and thoughtless way of going through life which has been developed out of our doctrine of individualism. The whole structure of our American scene has thus far been built on the theory that if you will only leave a man to himself, allow him freely to exercise his own God-given initiative, protect him through school and college from all religious propaganda, while exposing him to every other sort under heaven, and send him out finally into the world with a few legal safeguards on his honesty and no limit to the wealth he can accumulate, you'll have in the end a lovely democratic state full of plenty and brotherhood. We are face to face in our day with some of the results. No amount of philan-

105

thropy, for which we are so justly or unjustly famous here in America, can serve to disguise the fundamental selfishness and thoughtlessness which motivate nine-tenths of our behavior.

I remember being approached some time ago on behalf of a huge page of religious advertising to be issued by one of our great daily newspapers. Every Saturday, week after week, it was to carry the caption, "Come to Church Tomorrow." Social and financial leaders, leaders in civic life and corporations, were to carry the expense and be listed as patrons. So was the influence of the gospel to be extended, figures proved it, and the strongest of all bulwarks strengthened against the menace of communism, socialism, and crime. It had come to this: Christianity, as it was put to me very frankly, was to be hawked about to help maintain an order that may conceivably need changing; it was to be promoted partly because of its economic value as a kind of burglar-protection; and by far the most effective way to keep it before the public in its present state of health was by means of an advertising campaign!

Here was no spontaneous product of a fine enthusiasm for the Christian religion; no great crusade in the name of humanity and of a loving, healing Christ; no stirring adventure that men were making individually and collectively toward the kingdom of God in the world; no irresistible sweep and rhythm, filling the churches by the clean impact of zealous lives one by one on other lives: if it had been, I too could have managed one of these New Testament "hosannas" and a "blessed be God!" Here, admittedly, was an attempt on the part of certain organized groups to promote religion as a policy in order to safeguard their own interests!

Such a story needs only to be told. It's just one other illustration of the workings of a fundamentally selfish and thoughtless and unchristian social order. All talk of religion is fruitless unless we begin deliberately making some headway against that underlying, popular mood. This primary urge to self-interest, of which they tell us we shall never rid human life, and on which we have built the complicated structure both of our own lives and of human society, is not only inadequate to bear the weight we have set upon it; in our more thoroughly articulated world it has come to show itself appallingly and quite promptly suicidal! The times are gone when a man's regard for himself could be allowed with comparative safety to take first place, with its attendant ill-will, distrust, and suspicion;

while his regard for others could be left over in the realm of experimental virtue! Robinson Crusoe, on a desert island with Friday, was under no great compulsion as far as the development of right social attitudes was concerned; but we are living too closely to one another for that. With us the fabric of life is being knit together more and more firmly under our very eyes every passing day. With us the establishment of right attitudes between individuals has come to mark the difference between continuance and disaster. It's that or nothing. What position one should take with regard to profit; with regard to the holding and administration of personal property; with regard to other races and other religions, we think these matters are fit subjects for discussion; they still lie in the area of debate. We are fools and blind not to see that in our kind of world they have already arrived on the field of action! With the disintegration of all we love best threatening us around the next corner, we haven't as much leisure as we used to spend in talking about economic justice and international good will! "Quit all that and do something," writes James. Let's at least realize that we have come to that stage! Selfishness and thoughtlessness are played out.

The second inadequate way of behaving in these days is what I am going to call the customary and imitative. It characterizes the habit-ridden individual who takes what has been handed down from the past and wants to go on with it world without end. As between nations he still prates in eighteenth century language about entangling foreign alliances. He still defines charity as a dole to beggars. He still calls the building of a library or a hospital out of ill-gotten gains philanthropy. He still thinks that the possession of property is a divine right instead of a right that inheres in society itself. What he does therefore in the way of contributing to the general need he does as a gesture of lofty compassion, with very little sense of obligation about it. He howls when he's taxed to take care of the poverty he refuses to remedy voluntarily, and because his people have always been patriotic, passes by in silence the fact that eighty or ninety cents on every dollar he pays the government still goes not to relief, nor to education, nor to the common weal, but to war!

You and I are to think these things through, that's all. We are not to be governed simply by what our fathers have thought, even if they did write the Declaration of Independence and the Constitution of the United States! It's just conceivable that a score or more of the notions we have inherited may be quite wrong and mischievous, and it wouldn't be the first time in history that that had happened! Custom is good, but we dare not be slaves to it. Loyalty is good, and necessary. But loyalty by itself spells nothing more than stagnation; on the basis of it there has to be a constant individual adventure.

We must be brave enough then to come to this: that even imitative behavior is inadequate, with all behavior by rule and rote, even though the person you try to imitate be Christ himself, and the rules you try to follow be rules you think you have deduced from the New Testament!

The fact is, and here I get hold of the real point which I should like to drive home if I can: the fact is that Jesus wasn't interested in life that is imitative, or whenever it acts wants to look up the procedure. He was interested in life that would follow, not copy Him, and by its faith let itself be made instinct with his spirit.

We have heard a great deal in recent years about the traditional morality of the Christian religion—how out of date it is. The Ten Commandments were adapted to the needs of a wandering nation of primitive people. The Sermon on the Mount was intended for a simple rural community. Neither of them, they tell us, can be forced to fit into the life of the twentieth century. The trouble with such careless statements is the failure of those who make them to realize that all morality which is purely traditional is always out of date! Christian conduct, when it becomes Christ-like, is creative. It hasn't its solitary spring and source in any ancient regulation. That's why Jesus was so wary of special rules, and so insistent on the great principles that had to underlie all behavior. Christian conduct has its spring and source equally in the past and present, in a dynamic and in-dwelling spirit. That's the centre and heart of the gospel: Christ, and the harmony which he and he alone can bring about between our lives here and the loving, eternal, creative will of God!

And you can't short-circuit that process, as one of our prominent clergymen tried to do again the other day, by laying your first emphasis on social reform. He was speaking of the effort the Church had been making to salvage human life from sin by preaching the power of Jesus Christ to redeem men one by one, and he said it was leaving people cold. It wasn't touching the world in

which they live. It wasn't talking the language of today. It was the
voice of a bygone age. And it would never prevent our western
civilization from going over the abyss.

That kind of loose talk is a sharp blade which cuts humanity's
throat! The hope of this world lies in the mind of Christ which
only the redeemed can ever have; it lies in folk who because they
themselves have been saved are "conscripts of the mighty dream"
to save mankind! The hope of this world lies in men and women
who will come at every fresh situation, at every strange new choice
which life thrusts upon them, with the freshness and originality,
the vision and courage of souls that by faith in him are Christ-
possessed, not striving slavishly and with difficulty to do what they
think is right—that's where our present futility and weakness root
themselves—but giving scope and passage to another will, quite
different from our own, a will that doesn't have to go around tire-
somely attempting to model the future on the past, but Christ-like
each day is quite capable of creating a new heaven and a new
earth!

We are told that Charles Dickens was haunted, waking and sleeping, by the characters that throng his books. In "David Copper-
field" he tells us so himself, counting over the faces that peer out
at him from the fleeting crowd: Pickwick, Micawber, Sam Weller,
Oliver Twist, Tiny Tim. So there have been lives in which a life
from Nazareth has been lived again, haunted waking and sleeping
by a spirit that isn't content to copy, but create! "Christ liveth
in me"; and Paul tramps a highway for the king of kings across
the Roman empire! "Christ liveth in me"; and Luther stands up
defiantly in a world that's strangely free! "Christ liveth in me";
and Albert Schweitzer steps down from the organ and follows
the voice of one who calls him to Igome in equatorial Africa. It
takes courage, yes; and it takes vision, to go where that Christ
wants us to follow him in this new world that's building.

Here is one coming at life creatively; listen to him:

> For my feet have stood upon the mountains,
> And I have seen a vision of beauty;
> And though my heart be cast down again,
> Yet will I lift up mine eyes unto the heavens;
> For he that worketh in heaven
> Worketh also in me;

As he hath lifted up the mountains,
So will he lift up my soul,
That I may behold the beauty of his work in the
    heavens.
And on the earth in the hearts of men.

Come now. Here is your past, with many an old problem in it that has never been solved: bereavements out of which you have never yet made anything; disappointments, failures, weariness, lying around waiting to be fashioned into something. Here in the present are misgivings and uncertainties, difficulties for which no one seems able to supply any adequate remedy, decisions you have to make without any precedent to guide you. Here around you is a world unutterably complicated and confused and askew, with situations turning up every day which nobody else in any age had to meet. What's your equipment? One woman facing it all told me that her equipment, and she seemed quite satisfied, was a Christianity that consisted in doing the best she could, saying her prayers, and going to church occasionally! What's yours?

"Be ye doers of the word, not hearers only." It was an odd trick of language among the Greeks that made doers and poets the same. There is a painting by Alma-Tadema called a "Reading from Homer." From a cool marble seat that forms a half-circle against the background of the distant sea leans forward the graceful figure of a young man, a garland wound about his brow, his face aglow with the light of memory; while around him a few choice spirits, having settled themselves comfortably for the long afternoon, listen spellbound to those deathless melodies of line and word that seem to fly full-winged from his lips. There is something enervating about the romance of it. Something almost insidious about its loveliness. The lad in front especially, lying prone on the sun-flecked pavement, his chin cupped in his hand, seems to embody in himself the loitering ease of the whole scene. But living is more, writes James, than the hearing of quick deeds and eager heroisms; more than the flowing music of majestic cadences, whether Moses uttered them or Homer, Pindar or Christ. Quit your sitting there just drinking it all in. You don't have to be the audience all the time! There is life! And here is this creative mind of Christ! Try your hand!

IF THAT SHOULD EVER HAPPEN TO ME—

WHEN GOD STANDS BY

They shall put you out of the synagogues: yea, the time cometh, that whosoever killeth you will think that he doeth God service.

JOHN xvi:2

I REMEMBER one afternoon watching the Bremen steam out of the placid harbor at Cherbourg into the black maw of a hurricane, white and majestic in one last gleam of sunlight before the tumult closed in and blotted her out of sight. That's what was happening to the men who sat listening to Jesus in the quiet of that last evening around the table. They were destined shortly, all of them, to face the wind and the dark. Whatever problem is posed for the human mind and heart by the existence of evil in a world of God, they were headed for it: not theoretically, as one would stage an academic debate, back and forth; but quite practically, behind prison bars and at the point of a sword! Things had been running smoothly enough thus far. Tomorrow on the hill there would be a cross, and life would start going bitterly wrong, as at a signal. It would seem like a ghastly world for such good people, with nothing much but contempt and death waiting around every corner, and God just standing by doing nothing. No matter how kind they were, putting themselves out to bring a little happiness on the earth, they'd be slapped in the face for their pains. Many a time they would look up amazed and hurt and bewildered. He only hoped they wouldn't be unsteadied by it. Perhaps if they remembered then how he had told them of it before, that would help. And it did. I am sure of it. Life might go bitterly wrong, but it wasn't bitterly inane and senseless. He had understood it. Jesus had at least put them on their guard against the savage ills of living!

And so I have planned that we shall all draw up our chairs together in front of this same distressing reality. Our experience of life's bitterness, maybe, is not so poignant as the apostles'; and yet I dare say it's poignant enough for our taste. It's still a rather ghastly place at times—this world which the creative will of God sent spinning down the ages; and we aren't always so confident that there is anything very friendly about it. It doesn't look like an arrangement with which even a human father could be well-pleased, with its sin and its pain and its sorrows that pile themselves up in a black mass making "their wide entreaty to the sky." Oscar Wilde used to say there was enough suffering in any lane in London to prove that God doesn't love the world: disease and poverty and lust and anxiety and gruelling disappointment and plenty of graves about! What in heaven's fair name can anybody make of it? And of him, if there is such a one, who stands by and allows it, and too often by ten times doesn't seem to turn his hand? Why? From the very cross itself tortured humanity flings its amazement in the face of that eternal silence: "My God, my God, why hast Thou forsaken me?"

Of course, I don't want to overstate the facts. We shouldn't, any of us. There's no use going on about them, as St. Augustine does in his Meditations, calling life wretched and blind and confused and unclean, the mistress of all evils, with death at her heels. I submit that life isn't only that. There is loyalty too in the world, there are homes, and laughter, and friendship, and music, and love; far more of these than some of us seem to think, and in odd corners too! You remember the legend about a certain Oriental king who was very unhappy, and summoned a philosopher to ask a little advice. The philosopher told him to seek out the most contented man in the kingdom, and to wear for a while his shirt. But when, after exhaustive investigation, they found the man, as you will have surmised, he had no shirt! There is happiness about in odd corners, and the beauty that makes for it; nor is anything cheaper: sunsets, flowing water, the virgin green of the spring, gentle hands. Even pain itself has its uses now and then, giving us a red light to keep us from disaster—to put us on our guard! No sense in passing all this up just because you want to make out a case against the love of God! Maybe he does give a star, as Swinburne says, only to take a sun away; but let's at least be honest about the stars! There are myriads of them! Why, I am told that in even the brute creation, where Nature is so frankly and undisguisedly red in tooth and claw, there is a balance that has to be set down on the credit side of the account, a kind of surplus about the joy of living over and above the pain of dying. And this I know: that if it weren't for the anguish that men cause themselves and each other the whole world of human life would wear a different face! No, we shall not paint the picture with colors that are too sombre. We mustn't misrepresent the facts.

But it does no good to understate them either, or to overlook them, as some folk want to do, smiling at them as if they weren't there! Pain is real enough, and all the host of ills that flesh is heir to. Nor is there any ready facile answer a man can give to them: grief-stricken eyes that look at you and want to know what sense Life makes, with a husband lying there dead, or a son who maybe would be better off so, or a poor racked body that goes on living just to be one long agony knocking at the doors of the mind behind the forehead, or a job that's gone now, and feet that ache, trudging the streets, never catching up with anything.

God pity the man who has only something light and merry to give them for their woe! If they are going to stand up at all they don't want a reed shaken by the wind. And they don't particularly want to hear what anybody has to say who is clothed in soft raiment. They that wear soft clothing are in king's houses. Let them be. But Jesus has something to say. He's their kind—a gallant guest at Life's feast where for him too the chief bounty was bitterness. When we set ourselves to face this problem of evil in a world of God, let's at least face it with his poised mind, not heightening any of the colors, and not toning them down either: just trying to be honest with Life, and with ourselves, and with that other who stands by. "They shall put you out of the synagogues: yea, the time cometh, that whosoever killeth you will think that he doeth God service."

Now to make any headway in this matter at all, we have to start out with an assumption. It's only an assumption. You reserve the right to make any other that seems more reasonable to you. It's the assumption that human souls are here to grow into some fitting stature: that this isn't the end of us; to put it simply, that we are getting ready for something. I dare say that has been said in your hearing more than once. Perhaps more than twice. But if you put even to God the same question every time things go wrong, he has to make you the same answer! Three multiplied by three is still nine, no matter how often you pose me the problem. No use telling a lie for variety's sake! Whenever you look up hurt and amazed and bewildered, the first stay to get hold of, like a man reaching for a strap when the subway lurches, is just that whatever else Life is, if it's interested in anything, it's interested in what you turn out to be. There is no other hypothesis I know of on which it can be made even to seem intelligible.

It isn't particularly interested in how long you live, that much is certain. As D. H. Lawrence once remarked, "Poor old Queen Victoria had length of days; but Emily Brontë had life. She died of it!" And there doesn't seem to be much concern anywhere that you should be, as we say, happy. Lawrence goes on: "Life is like a capricious mistress: the more you woo her, the more she despises you. You have to get up and go to something more interesting. Then she'll pelt after you." It's concerned, this strange business of living, with what you become, and it will take off its hat to you in the end if you grow to some decent height. The men at the front during the War came to feel that way about it. They said in effect, as their well-nigh unanimous answer to a questionnaire that was circulated among them, "There is something going on in the world which demands primarily allegiance. We hardly know what it is. We only know that something great and righteous wants us and requires of us our help." Behind all the cruel folly of war they could feel that! You may try all the other conclusions you like; but you'll come back to this: that the supreme issue of living is the state of a human soul!

When once that has taken firm hold of you, there can be little doubt left that some kind of struggle in a neutral, perhaps even a seemingly hostile world, is going to prove inevitable. Moral struggle is the price Life has to pay somehow for progress. A "comfortable" world is no place for the growth of a sturdy spirit. Dr. Swan, of the Franklin Institute in Philadelphia, used to say that he could imagine no more perfect hell for an atheist than having to live in the kind of vacant and purposeless universe that all atheism presupposes. I can imagine no more perfect hell for the staunch stuff of which humanity is made than a flabby world that would never confront anybody with grief or disappointment or pain or quick disaster. I can't picture such an order with men in it, with courage in it, or faith in it, or sacrificial love in it, or anything in it that makes a man a man! Why Almighty God didn't fix it so that we could have victory without the possibility of defeat, bravery without any reason for fear, peace without any necessity for tumult

—I don't know. It's about as reasonable as to suggest that we should
have been blessed with the kind of fire that can broil a steak but
can't burn down a house. I only know that a being who is incapable
of pain would be incapable of joy, and no man at all; if words have
any meaning and thought has any significance. I only know that
a man incapable of wrong would be incapable of right; or else
humanity would no longer be humanity, and the mind would be
no longer the mind. This world may not seem to you the best of
all possible worlds; but I hazard the statement that it's the best
of all possible worlds for the growth of a human soul! I at least
have trouble trying to fashion any other!

But more than that: when the plain truth is spoken we like the
hazards. Our interest too "is on the dangerous edge of things."
If there aren't any perils around we either manufacture a few, or
we go and get our thrills vicariously at the movies, or we are bored
stiff. And that's a fact! The trouble with what we call dead cer-
tainties, as someone has put it, seems to be just that: they're dead!
Surely all the truest and the highest and the noblest that's in us
goes out in solemn salutation to every divine flash of heroism that
lightens the drab landscape of the world. Scott wrote home from
the dreary wastes of Antarctica: "My dear Sir Edgar, I hope this
reaches you. We have been to the Pole and we shall die like gen-
tlemen. We very nearly came through, and it's a pity to have missed
it. If this diary is found it will show how we stuck by dying companions and fought the thing out until the end." When that diary
was found there wasn't a heart in the civilized world that didn't
stand at salute; because we knew very well that something great
was passing by!

And really it was only another form of the heroism that grew
on my street one day in the humble heart of a mother who lingered
by the dead body of her husband, dedicating all the years that were
left to the lad, a man now, who waited there with her, his hand
in hers, his wide eyes quite innocent of the world's threat and of
the lone flag that fluttered against it. Again our souls stand at
salute. Without knowing altogether why I can understand that
William James was right when he said that "Life is an austere
tragedy in which we relish most the bitterest it has to offer. On
the scene of the world heroism alone plays the great parts. In it
lies the hidden mystery of life. A man is nothing if he is incapable

of sacrifice. Evident though his shortcomings may be, if he is ready to give up his life, we forgive him everything. However inferior he may be to us in other respects, if we cling to life while he throws it away like a flower, we bow to his superiority."

"They shall put you out of the synagogues: yea, the time cometh, that whoever killeth you will think that he doeth God service." There was the fact then, and they were not to brood over it! They were to realize this, that the first solution of the problem of evil in a world of God lies in an act of the human will. There is no end to it until a man draws his sword. Jacob found that out wrestling there with his fear and his God by the river's edge, crying aloud in his extremity, "I will not let Thee go except Thou bless me"; and in the morning as the sun rose he halted upon his thigh, moving on through the fantastic garlands of the mist toward a new day. Job found it out, as he struggled to his feet against the torrent of words his friends poured out upon him, and fairly shouted, "Hold your peace, let me alone, that I may speak, let come on me what will . . . Though he slay me, yet will I trust him." And the psalmist found it out, as he mulled over in his memory the deadliest things on earth, then broke away to the glory and goodness of God: "Thy mercy, O Lord, is in the heavens; and Thy faithfulness reacheth unto the clouds." It's amazing how often we meet with that gallant recoil in the case of those who suffer deeply. It's the peevish fellow with little sorrows who makes the angriest complaint. So may a man learn to fling ahead against the most savage of life's ills, with a faith in God's good will that makes them look tame!

Then, and only then, when our spirits leap free against the world, do we discover that God is standing by, not as one who looks on and does nothing, but as one ready to run up at a gesture and throw down all he has. Because, you see, he has been in this too! Not Mr. Jeans' mathematical God, who might cause a sparrow's fall, but could never mark it with compassionate eyes; but the God who was in the gentlest man that ever lived and was crucified for it; the kindest friend anyone ever had, and was betrayed for it, with thirty pieces of silver clinking coldly in a leather bag God has been in the midst of all human tears. He lost his son there A friend of mine once said, speaking of his own son that was killed, "If I had lost my son and God had not lost his, I should

have had a depth of experience denied even to God Himself!"
There is one who came over on our side of the gulf, and picked
up somehow worse scars than mine. Our tragedies are light against
the darkness of his cross. I think he has a right now to take all
weary folk in his arms, and say to them great, tender, knowing
words, and not let them go. Calvary is the last comfort God has
to give when Life throws all its weight against a man! And isn't
it enough? Isn't it enough?

THE FRIENDLY DARK

I will give thee the treasures of darkness.

ISAIAH xlv:3

IF YOU have any imagination left in you at all after another week's experience of traffic lights and what-not; if the telephone, especially the dial-telephone, has overlooked a little something that's poetic in your soul, and allowed it to linger on; I think you will agree that this word of the prophet Isaiah is simply magnificent: "I will give thee the treasures of darkness." It doesn't mean what it says, in case anybody is prosaic enough to want to know what it means! God is promising Cyrus, king of Persia, all the hidden wealth of Babylon in return for the deliverance of Israel out of exile. That's the history—for curious people! But we shall not allow ourselves to be embarrassed by the facts! It's quite too striking a phrase, "the treasures of darkness," to have it go limping along under the burden of what it meant 2500 years ago. Let us give it wings for its feet!

Deep inside of us, I suppose, it has always been the light that we have thought of, instinctively, as friendly: we've never given the dark any real credit. Even the Bible doesn't. You will find that out if you look up the word. It has always stood for bewilderment, and hopelessness, and sin: the sweet and healing balm of it, its slow creative fingers away where seeds grow secretly in its womb— these things have never impressed us much. We are still prehistoric cavemen, and watch the sun go down with prehistoric shuddering, slinking into caves and building fires against our prehistoric enemy, the Dark!

It's very tragic, and very slanderous. A young mother once told me what she was doing about it, taking every evening her six-months'-old child in her arms up the steps, away from the light, that some day it might learn to reach out its hands in welcome to the friendly shadows,

> The dark that's kind and silent,
> The dark that's soft and deep;

The dark that smoothes the pillow,
And watches as men sleep.

"Our enemy, the Dark!" It's slander, you know. The grass knows
it, on a thousand hills, burned all day by the sun, until it droops,
weary and thirsty for the night again. David knew it, as the west
turned crimson, then grey, and out across the plains of the sky
marched the uncounted stars. It was only then that he sang, "When
I consider the heavens, the work of thy fingers; the moon and the
stars, which thou hast ordained; what is man, that thou art mindful
of him. . . . ?" There is a majesty from which the day would keep
us. It has ever taken the falling of a mantle on the earth to reveal
these other thoughts of God in the Universe beyond. Yes, we should
have seemed quite alone without the night! Perhaps that's what's
the matter with Broadway, Market or Main Street or Michigan
Avenue; always, always day there, and the poor corners that keep
waiting for the dark, and nobody can find anything, or God, in
the glare of a million bulbs! "I will give thee the treasures of darkness." There's a sermon in it, I'm sure of that, whether it comes
out or not! "The Friendly Dark."

Could we think of these last years in some such fashion, I wonder?
If anything in this world ever wore the look of black and bleak
disaster, they did! Frederick Allen, in his book "Only Yesterday"
has written of them: a decade of jazz and sex, of crime and over-
production, sport, and ballyhoo; until paralysis came, paralysis
which we are unable even to diagnose, hunger in the midst of
plenty, unemployment "in the face of an unparalleled need of the
very commodities" which our "factories were clamoring to produce."
"Ours is an age," wrote another, "that would stand condemned
by all the foremost teachers and prophets from the beginning of
history. Socrates would riddle it with scorn. Jesus would have none
of it. Buddha—there is not one to whom it would not seem repel-
ent and unclean." He was a brave man who talked of assets.

And yet—were they ever talked of more than through the last
months or shall I say years of that grim experience? Wherever
you turned there was some sober effort at appraisal; until smartness
didn't seem so popular any more. I still remember reading in the
midst of it all a book on psychology in which God and the soul
came in for honorable mention! On the 30th of December, 1931,

after a long absence, sin was referred to in one of our great religiou weeklies. "The experience of the past," it declared, "has giver convincing proof of a mistaken estimate of human nature. W have made men believe that a little more education and anothe sermon or two on love would produce the kingdom of God." An somehow it seemed queerly refreshing, like the return of sanit to a mind that had wandered! Here, coming on down the list, wa a daily newspaper, as it wrote its summary of that same year: "Th gains of the last twelve months have been the gains of men who suddenly bereft of the familiar reliances, turned with some earnest ness to things that are not material. In deprivation, in suffering in desperation, they have developed resources . . . neglected i softer times. There is not the slightest doubt that millions of cha tened men and women survey with gratitude new domes and tower that fill in their mental and spiritual sky-lines." And that editio was sold out as soon as it reached the newsstands! "I will give the the treasures of darkness." It isn't only optimism. In all earnestnes with a matter-of-fact sobriety, we may begin entering a few item at last on the credit-side of the ledger! Listen to another writin of the challenge that Life has thrown at our feet: "It is not securit that develops the human spirit, but danger. Not in hours of placic ity do men build a Chartres Cathedral, or paint the frescoes in th Sistine Chapel, or write a constitution in Independence Hall . . Change is a phase of progress; decay is a prerequisite to growth . . If prosperity means only houses and furniture, automobiles an refrigerators, and no life that transcends them all, then let us pra that the blight may never return. A new adventure is beginnin, a new search; perhaps, who knows?—a new Renaissance! We strik our tents!"

But all of that is in such general terms, and I want here to b specific. I want to take your life and get you to look at it. I war you especially to go peering about in its shadows. It's all very we to talk in large world-figures of the good that's been coming ou of our wide and bitter discipline; but how about your case? Noboc has written any articles about that! And you wonder sometim how long you can hold on, with the anxiety. Or perhaps it's som kind of bereavement, or illness somewhere, or disappointmen and the day isn't very much brighter than the night; it's all a indistinguishable grey!

So it is, if you sit down in it, and let it envelop you. Here comes God with his whispering: "I will give thee the treasures of darkness." And you wait there wondering when he's going to begin pouring them into your lap! Who wants to sit still in the dark, trying to put up with it, when all around there is wealth for the seeking?

In the dark, for the first time, a man may find his soul. You remember the story of The Blind Ploughman:

> Set my hands upon the plough,
> My feet upon the sod:
> Turn my face then toward the East,
> And praise be to God!
>
> The God that made his sun to shine
> Alike on you and me;
> The God who took away my eyes,
> That now my soul might see.

And the spiritual counterpart of it is in this description I came upon recently which a British man of letters gives of the career of one of his friends: "He had to bear a series of devastating calamities. He had loved the warmth and nearness of his home-circle more than most men, and the whole of it was swept away; he had depended for both stimulus and occupation upon his artistic work, and the power was taken from him at the moment of his highest achievement. But his loss of fortune is not to be reckoned among his calamities, because it was no calamity to him. He ended by finding a richer treasure than that he had set out to obtain; and I remember that he said to me once, not long before the end, that whatever others might feel about their lives, he could not for a moment doubt that his own had been an education of a deliberate and loving kind, and that the day when he realized that, when he saw that there was not a single incident that had not a deep and intentional value for him, was one of the happiest days of his whole existence. "I will give thee the treasures of darkness."

In the dark for the first time a man may find God. More discoveries have been made there by far than in the light. It was where George Matheson made his; after the love of a woman had loosened its hold: there, waiting, but never clearly seen before, the Love that would not let him go. "Come and find me," God seems to say, and lures us through to vision. And that faith, writes another, which we have found for ourselves in the darkness, is ours as no light-hearted, casual creed can ever be. "I had heard of thee by the hearing of the ear," confessed Job, as he came up out of his long and darkly shadowed valley: "but now mine eye seeth thee." That night before the crucifixion, when bread was broken and a cup went round the circle, there was a presence in the room; clouds and thick darkness along all the ways of life, but peace here, and God! All through the deep and ominous shadows of a changing world, this one went with them; and down through the ages his saints salute us! You think life is hard, they say to us, and the way dark: reach out your hands as we did; God is there. In the day, we followed our sight: in the night we had to follow his; and we traveled farther in the night, and there was less stumbling. Jerusalem fell and was sacked. It seemed like the end. But we learned that the winds which blew were the winds of God. Heathen hordes poured in from the North, and we thought the world we knew would disappear, and the Church with it, and all our faith. But it was God's Dark. Again in the Reformation it fell; in the days of the French Revolution. There were upheavals without end, social political, intellectual. Bewildered, are you? So were we, times any number. Good Companions in the life with Christ, courage! God is in the friendly Dark!

"I will give thee the treasures of darkness."

"Friendly Dark" did I say? Creative Dark—where seeds grow and God sets away his bulbs to flower!

ROUND ABOUT BY WAY OF THE WILDERNESS

And it came to pass, when Pharaoh had let the people go, that God led them not through the way of the land of the Philistines, although that was near; . . . but God led the people about through the way of the wilderness.

EXODUS xiii:17,18

A STRAIGHT line is the shortest line between two points; but it's not always the best road to travel! In the old days, when you left New England, or Virginia, or some other state along the Atlantic Seaboard, for the West, as so many of our ancestors did, you took a horse or two, and a covered wagon, and followed the river beds, skirting the mountains, winding in and out as the land lay: and it took you months to make the trip. But you learned a good deal en route. You overcame many hardships, and weathered many privations. When you arrived, if you did arrive, you weren't just the same person who set out: you had been equipped by the journey itself, and hardened into some sort of fitness for your new life on the prairies.

Today, you step into an airplane. You follow a much straighter line. You fly as the crow flies, and it takes you only a few hours. But the trip does you no good! You're just as feeble-minded in Los Angeles when you get out as you were in New York when you got in; no more, no less. You've saved time, and covered ground; but what of it? You haven't added anything much to your fund of usable experience. You have accumulated no capital assets really. Other things being equal, you'd be just as well off if you were back where you started!

Now the fact is, of course, that these Israelites simply weren't ready for the Promised Land. If they had been led there promptly and directly, they would have been slaves still, precisely as they were when they came out of Egypt. And between a slave by the Jordan and a slave by the Nile, there wasn't much choice. What they needed was time in which to become a nation. The shortest road was not for them the best; there was no use traveling it: there was more, much more, to be had round about through the way of the wilderness. Some day, when they arrived, they'd be fit. So off they struck toward the east; because God was quite sure that was the only road that would take them north adequately! They were to go from A to B, but they were to go through Z! They would be different people when it was over!

It's a necessity with which we are often faced, this business of going around. Anybody who has ever lived close to life will tell you that trying to save time by taking short-cuts is one of the most perilous things folk do. Humanity has thrown up half-a-dozen proverbs on the subject that float around now on the surface of every generation, bearing witness to the miserable hours leisure has had in which to repent of haste! "Look before you leap," for instance, is all that's left of thousands who shut their eyes, jumped on impulse, and landed in the mire. "Think twice before you speak" is the only remnant of other thousands who blurted out something helter-skelter one day to avoid the harsh exactions of thought, and wound up under an avalanche of trouble. "There's no royal road to learning" sadly commemorates all the scholars in correspondence schools who have attempted to learn French or the piano in six easy lessons. It's the distilled wisdom of a good many ages that keeps warning us against this too great eagerness of ours to get somewhere without being very careful to fill up the spaces in between! There is a sort of immediacy about the American character which only succeeds in turning most of us into mushrooms that spring up over night, when we were really intended to be oaks!

Certainly, there is another side of the picture. Dr. Hutton insists on it in one of his essays. There are times, and nobody can afford to leave them out of the reckoning, when our first thoughts are our best thoughts, and "delays are dangerous"; when the short-cut is God's way of traveling; when to think again is to spoil the quick, generous motions of the soul; when to hesitate is to allow some lower motive to creep in and crowd out the "momentary gleam," and the sudden beauty. But I am deliberately setting all that aside: you can't ride a horse, or a sermon either, in all directions at once! Let's stick to our peril: this "eventually, why not now?" doctrine of the twentieth century, which goes about hurrying things that won't be hurried! It makes a dive at sobriety and temperance by cutting across through prohibition, and like Christian and his friend Hopeful in "Pilgrim's Progress," discovers that the By-path ends in a bog presided over by the castle of Giant Despair! We, too made our acquaintance with the Giant, and came near being consumed by him! Or a whole civilization, shall we say, bewildered by injustice and all the sly devices of human greed, leaps as it did in Russia, towards fairness and decency, only to find itself caught in the toils of a wretched tyranny scarcely if at all better than the old. Life rarely ever moves to any lasting profit or advantage with such spontaneity and suddenness. Again and again, all out of breath by reason of some thoughtless venture, painstakingly it has to retrace its steps, until it comes to the stile where one day it turned aside to save itself time; and then setting its feet surely once more on the long, clear road, it straightens its shoulders for the journey. "God led them not through the way of the land of the Philistines, although that was near; . . . but round about through the way of the wilderness."

Shall we keep holding this in view then, as one of the simple, profound truths which help to shape all human destiny? Jesus came face to face with it in his own person, as he stood yonder on the threshold of his ministry, and a voice whispered: "Cast thyself down; for it is written, he shall give his angels charge concerning thee; in their hands shall they bear thee up, lest at any time thou dash thy foot against a stone." There was the dark and sinister suggestion that he get on with it: to clutch all his faith in his hands, and with one wild hazard show the crowds loitering in the temple courts what mighty things this God could do! To win them at a stroke, without the years, and the pain, and the dust, and the cross at the end! But he kept shaking his head, and looking distantly into the future, his lips moving quietly: "Not near! Not near! Round about through the way of the wilderness!"

I wonder if that has anything to say to you and me here today? There are experiences a-plenty that are quite like the desert. I wonder if they are God's way around? Maybe that's what age is, feeling itself so useless, asking its constant questions about the purpose of it all. God's way around! And this recent harshness that living seems to have acquired. A friend said to me the other evening, "Even you, close as you have been to me these last years, can never know what I owe God, back of the loss and the anxiety, the hurt and the dryness." God's way—around!

I suppose that nobody has been having exactly a smooth time of it lately; though as I have often said, I hope we aren't exaggerating the roughness. That would be just blind folly and ingratitude, to magnify a few normal difficulties, and a little average hardship, and call the sum of it a desert, when really it was nothing more than a cross-country hike! But we have known something of life's apparent sternness, haven't we? How carelessly it seems to narrow us down sometimes, and take things away that we thought quite necessary. The income we used to have is the least of it. Maybe it's the health we had, or the hope we had, or even some love we had. And it's gone now. And the road is lonelier and there hardly seems to be anything much worth having anywhere on the horizon. It gets to be dreadfully poignant now and then, going on that way so long with no heart for it any more. There are some who under the stress of it are willing to throw away all of the future, grab God's purposes out of his hand, chuck them all on the dust-heap, and rush unbidden out of life. They just won't travel God's way around! I heard the other day of one who was worse than a murderer, as Chesterton once put it, because in killing himself he had killed the whole world beside; and in the mails that evening came a letter offering him a position at some seven thousand a year!

It's the postponements we seem unable to bear: that we should have to wait for marriage and friendship, for experience, and success, and whatever plan God has; that we should have to wait for everything to ripen as he wants it. We'd rather snatch it and bend it, or warp it or break it, on some blue devil of a day, and grow bitter or sour, impatient, resentful, out of breath. Here, on the side of our faith, these promises of God range themselves, and all that we dream of his kingdom in the world; and today and tomorrow we run up to them. "See, Father, we are on our knees. Stand not ashamed now before thy word. Tarry no longer. Set thy face against greed, and injustice, and war, and all these things that clutch at us and drag us back. Why lookest thou on, and holdest thy tongue?" And we go plunging in, and tugging at it manfully, running back to him every morning, crying "Hurry! Hurry!" We do that until our hands are not only empty but sore. And nothing seems to budge. Would it save us anything, do you think, to remember then that maybe after all it's God's road we're on, and as often as not that road is long, and by the way of the wilderness!

You won't misunderstand me, will you? It isn't any mood of contentment I'd be commending to you: that a man should settle down with a sigh in this wretched world, or in the midst of his own failures, and do nothing but wait. That's a silly caricature of the truth. I am just hoping against hope that some of us may learn to wait better while we work!

Because that's the only way to the kind of victory which God meant for human souls to have! Not the kind you are after necessarily. The kind he's after! There are in the Bible no foolish promises for faithful people, half-way along some unwise course they have chosen for themselves, that things will turn out at last as they had planned. Pay no attention to anybody who says to you at commencement exercises:

> Upon the wreckage of thy yesterday
> Design thy structure of tomorrow. Lay
> Strong cornerstones of purpose and prepare
> Great blocks of wisdom cut from dark despair.
> Shape mighty pillars of resolve, to set
> Deep in the tear-wet mortar of regret.
> Believe in God—in thine own self believe:
> *All thou hast hoped for thou shalt yet achieve.*

It's a shame to fool young people on their graduation day! The Bible is too much of a realist to let you get away with that. The only assurance patience is heir to is the assurance of some crown that God has pledged himself to fashion, quite different it may be from any of which you happen to be thinking. I haven't the slightest idea what he has in mind for you. Nor has anyone else. I don't even know if what you're doing at the moment is on the road to it. I do know, and I have his word for this, that nothing on earth can keep you from it half so effectively as your own feverish haste and wilfulness.

It may just be—in fact, I myself see nothing else for it—that you and I are in this world, not so much to achieve something as to be something; and by that means, not another, to help bring the kingdom of God among men. I am not amazed at the time that takes. Being something always does take time; and tears, they may be a part of it; and broken hopes, and bitter delays. But surely, it is not these things that matter. What matters is the stature of the soul that comes through them: if it's mean, and wizened, and full of discontent; or poised and gracious, and quick with compassion!

Dr. Hutton, editor of the *British Weekly*, tells us that on the golf links at St. Andrew's the higher grade of caddie is something of a dictator. He hands you the proper club, gives you the direction, and then awaits in silence the event. One day a stranger, unacquainted with this delightful tyranny, reached the tee for a dog-leg hole, which had to be negotiated circuitously. The caddie handed him a club and said, "You play on that tar-roofed shed, away there to the left." "Would it not be better," objected the stranger, "to go straight for it?" To which the caddie retorted, "You may play in any direction you like; I was only suggesting how to play in order to win the hole."

And under that story, as under a text, our editor in his book sets down an incident from the life of St. Francis. Among the saint's companions was one, Brother Masseo, who fancied himself something of a preacher; and it rankled in his mind that he should be kept busy so long at some difficult and obscure work. Whereupon St. Francis, perceiving the struggle that was going on, said to him in effect: "Brother Masseo, I know your gifts. You have the qualities of a great preacher. But to sway these multitudes now would be to you a form of self-indulgence. I ordain therefore that you shall continue to act as porter to the lodge!"

"Not through the way of the land of the Philistines though that was near; but God led the people about through the way of the wilderness." On the other side of that, for all the murmuring they did, lay the land of his promise!

And to make it clear for us, there stands one near who came to a manger in Bethlehem. Thirty years he waited in a carpenter's shop. Even then it was no triumph to be won at a stroke. There was no crown to be had for a leap. His brothers and sisters shrugged their shoulders at him. One by one his friends left him. The storm blew up and broke. They nailed him to a cross, until the day came, and an empty tomb was behind him. Surely then this is the end and the victory! Not yet. He said to Simon, "Go and preach." "To the men that crucified thee, Lord?" "Yes." "To those that brought the crown of thorns?" "Yes. Say I still have my crown; and to him that came with the reed say that I shall have a sceptre, too!" "Preach, Lord, to the men who drove the nails?" "Yes. And to them that cursed say I have a song for them; and to the soldier who pierced my side say there's a nearer way to my heart than that!" It was God's road, and it was long and round about, and it ran far away, and out of sight, toward the spires on the world's rim!

THE PLACE OF UNDERSTANDING

Where shall wisdom be found? and where is the place of understanding? The depth saith, It is not in me: and the sea saith, It is not with me.

JOB xxviii:12,14

JOB had a problem on his hands. I am not particularly fond of the word problem. It has been rolled around on the tongue so long that it has lost its freshness. But I don't know of any other that I can use. After all, there is very little freshness about the fact itself: a problem is a problem, no matter if you go back as far on the other side of Christ as we are on this. And Job's problem was the problem of ill-health. The physical aspects of it didn't worry him a great deal: the moral aspects of it worried him tremendously. His orthodox friends told him he was being punished for his sins: for fifteen chapters they told him that, with ornamental variations. In what must have seemed like the boldest kind of irreverence, for twenty chapters he denied it. He could lie, but he wouldn't: his conscience was clear. That's what made it horrible: it seemed so senseless that he should suffer this way, for no reason! Back and forth he wrestled, between faith and doubt, hope and despair. It was a troubled mind that he had; which anybody knows is worse than a sick body!

There was no use going to Atlantic City or Daytona Beach: that much at least was apparent to him. He wasn't looking for "a complete rest, with plenty of salt air and good, wholesome food." For what ailed him, he needed wisdom most of all. He could scrape his boils, but he couldn't appease his own soul! And there is precisely the tragedy of the boardwalk: you have to take your soul with you! During a week or two at high prices you discover that the wild waves haven't the secret: "The sea saith, It is not with me"—as it comes roaring up on the beach only to slither back again in a dismal sort of futility! And perhaps after a while you begin to wonder why we are so often passionately intent on treating sick bodies, when it's the sick soul that needs treatment!

Take one or two of our modern human problems, for instance;

"modern" only in the sense that we have given some of them modern names. They are all as old as the hills, and just as real as mumps and measles, with a fatality curve that makes appendicitis and pneumonia look like innocent bystanders at an Armenian massacre!

First, there is funk; which is a kind of ingrowing fear that makes you "hectic and fussy and worried." You rarely or never do anything without misgivings, a torturing sort of terror that maybe it was the wrong thing, and something else would have been better! You are sure to get indigestion, and catch your neighbor's cold. You are in a clammy sweat because of what people are saying about you. There is something that has to be done, and you are dreading lest you can't make good.

Or perhaps it's frustration. That's a new name for an old disorder. You have never been able really to express yourself. You were an artist, and you had to be a clerk. You would have made somebody a good wife or a good husband; but somehow you never got around to it. You were married, and had no children. In one way or another, life has had very little fulfilment. You have met with meagre success. Circumstances have hemmed you in, and kept you from being the whole self you could have been. Until now the wind is out of your sails, and you go around trying to make up for it by being offensive. You could have been something too, if it hadn't been for the boils, or whatever it was that stopped you. Listen to Job:

"Oh that I were as in months past, in the days when God preserved me! The young men saw me, and hid themselves; the aged arose, and stood up. When the ear heard me, then it blessed me; when the eye saw me, it gave witness. After my words they spake not again. They waited for me as for the rain. . . . And now they have me in derision, whose fathers I would have disdained to set with the dogs of my flock. I am their song; yea, I am their byword." Is that the trouble? Just baffled?

Or perhaps it's conflict. There's another new way of saying an old thing. Some evil in your life is at war with your ideals. It makes you despise yourself. If you had no ideals, you'd have some peace; but it would be the peace of cattle and of pigs. Thank God you are not an animal! You have to have ideals. It's the price you pay for being a man! And so the fight goes on, between what you want to be and what you are, between your hope for the future and your failures of the past. You try to put the whole business out of your mind; but it trickles down on the lower levels, into the unconscious, and raises the mischief out of sight.

Now there is very little profit to be had out of taking that sort of self to the seashore, or getting into the great out-of-doors, or tucking a tennis racquet under its arm, or slinging a golf bag over its shoulder. There is very little profit to be had out of trying to forget about it, or going to the movies, or occupying your mind with something else. "The depth saith, It is not in me; and the sea saith, It is not with me." "Where shall wisdom be found?" That's what a man needs then! "And where is the place of understanding?"

You remember Macbeth, as he hears of his wife's growing delirium:

> How does your patient, Doctor?
>
>   Not so sick, my lord,
> As she is troubled with thick-coming fancies,
> That keep her from her rest.
>
>   Cure her of that.
> Canst thou not minister to a mind diseased;
> Pluck from the memory a rooted sorrow;
> Raze out the written troubles of the brain;
> And, with some sweet oblivious antidote,
> Cleanse the stuff'd bosom of that perilous stuff
> Which weighs upon the heart?

And he wasn't altogether wrong! There ought to be some medicine for the soul.

Some of us believe there is. We believe that the religion of Jesus Christ is just that; not at its highest, but at its lowest! It's intended at least to make sick people well—I mean people who are spiritually sick; after that, it's intended to make them strong and able, with the strength of God!

Job, back there on the other side of the centuries, was sure that the process began in the place which he called the place of understanding; and no modern psychologist has ever got any further. The only thing the last fifty years have added is a bit of technique.

By one device or another you are hauled back through dreams and hidden memories to the day when some simple, primary urge of your life went wrong: some desire, or fear, or hate, took the bit in its teeth and ran away; and there, if it comes at all, in the place of understanding, comes release! Here, at the close of this ancient book, God himself moves over into the picture, and the hope and despair which had been making Job's soul a battlefield laid down their arms. "The fear of the Lord, that is wisdom: and to depart from evil is understanding." And over the poor, scarred ground of a life that had learned to lift its face in unutterable trust fell, like the dawn of a clear day, the peace of God.

I do not believe that we have come beyond it. The longer one deals with human nature, and with all those disorders which make it so strange and difficult a thing, the more firmly is one convinced of the amazing relevancy, the almost incredible aptness, of the Christian religion. To my knowledge, I have never stumbled upon a single instance, either in my experience or in my reading, of anxiety, of restlessness, of what we call plain, ordinary "nerves"— not one that wasn't the result of flouting that religion, consciously or unconsciously; and not one the cure of which did not lie well within its province. Weatherhead, in his "Psychology in Service of the Soul," tells of a woman who came to him on the verge of a breakdown. She was in a pitiable state, manifesting all the physical symptoms of great distress. It was hard to get behind her mind to see what was the matter. But at last it came out. There had been a rift between herself and her brother. Natural love and acquired hate had set her soul in opposite camps, warring against itself. The solution of it, and of the sleepless nights that went with it, came as if by magic; but it wasn't magic: it was Christ's answer to Peter's question! "How oft shall my brother sin against me, and I forgive him? Till seven times?" And the secret was whispered back: "Seventy times seven!" She sat down and wrote her brother a letter, inviting him to her home, and the ugly chapter in her life came to its close.

It doesn't matter what sort of stress or strain it is that disturbs your peace. If it's some understanding of yourself that you need, Christ can bring you to that. He'll show you the worst, and then he'll tell you that that doesn't even begin to prejudice the best that he keeps talking about. If it's forgiveness, you may have that; if you'll just reach yonder and lay your hands on it, and know that you have it. When you put out an old sin that way, it's out. You don't just try to forget it, and so send it digging deeper down into your vitals: you get rid of it. It's gone! If it's courage you lack, because failure and disappointment and hopelessness have made you feel that you can't face life, then the only fight you have is the fight with your own doubts that "the mighty gifts of this God are yours for the taking!" Instead of simply looking at the idea of God's presence, and shaking your head piously, sniffing each Sunday at the aroma of orthodoxy, let your mind receive it. Practice throwing open the doors and allowing it to come in! That isn't easy. You need to work at it; more than offering desultory prayers, doing a bit of idle reading between the covers of a book, and singing a few hymns with one vocal cord and the top quarter of your lungs! These fears that haunt you: lie down quietly at night on your bed and for fifteen minutes say aloud to yourself, "In him that strengtheneth me, I am able for anything!" See what happens to them when you work at them, instead of spending all your time trying to cling by your finger-nails to what little religion you have left. I had a letter some time ago about a young man who is preparing for the ministry, and has been told that he is growing gradually but surely deaf; and another from a woman who sits looking into the thickening shadows of approaching blindness. Christianity is no facile optimist that comes to those two people and says with a foolish, vacuous smile, "Cheer up!" Christianity breaks its heart over them in an agony of hope, with its eyes wide open and wistful in the knowledge of what God can do with them in spite of it all if they'll let him! Let him, I repeat.

And so I come to the last word which this religion of ours has to say in the hearing of all troubled souls everywhere: give yourself somehow, somewhere, to that long, human cry for help which rings daily in God's ears. There are men and women in the world who are so busy healing the minds and bodies of other people that they have no time left in which to be mentally or spiritually sick themselves! It isn't without its significance that the sort of ill-health of which we have been thinking together so frequently goes hand in hand with those ways of life that do not occupy themselves very much in the service of other life. In moments of high devotion there is no room for brooding uneasiness. Last week a lifeboat was launched on pounding seas from the *S. S. Washington*. It pulled yonder to where five men were clinging to a wrecked plane. There was a call for volunteers to swim the remaining distance with a line: without waiting for any choice to be made two of the sailors were out of the boat and into the water. Do you think, if you had happened just then to be looking for a good old-fashioned case of what they call nowadays mental conflict, or frustration, or downright, home-spun funk, or nervous depression—if you had happened just then, in short, to be looking for a case to take to the psychiatrist: do you think you would have found it in either of those two, plowing through the waves with a line around their waist? "As the Father hath sent me, even so send I you." There isn't much time for being anything but well when folk are continuously about the biggest business there is in the world! Is that the answer?

STRENGTH MADE PERFECT IN WEAKNESS

My strength is made perfect in weakness.
II Corinthians xii:9

THAT'S the answer Paul got when he prayed about his thorn. It's enough for you to have my grace; my power makes itself fully felt when there is no other support.

Now a proper sermon should take that up and proceed along it for twenty minutes or so, as though it were an old acquaintance known to everybody; at the end one would withdraw into some conclusion, and likely enough run the risk of leaving the text itself like a perfect stranger on your doorstep, well analyzed, but never quite introduced! I want to say something here, if I can, that will serve no other purpose than to introduce the text.

Let me begin back yonder somewhere, with this: that the world is too strong for us. There's one of the secrets of life, like my text, that we're bound to wind up with. We learn it sooner or later by being battered about and growing old and dying. Why not get a running jump on living and start with it? The world is too strong for us!

I cannot see that anything is more manifest. One might almost be bold enough to say that there would never have been any religion at all if men and women, alone and unaided, had ever been able to cope successfully, in any real and vital fashion, with the victories and defeats and difficulties of this queer place where they have been set down to live their lives! The savage knew very well that he couldn't cope with them. And I dare submit to you today, in this year of our Lord 1938, that we aren't a great deal better off! The only mastery we have won is a sort of fictitious mastery that looks all right, but when things come to the pinch it doesn't honestly work; not if we are frank about it. We can protect ourselves from storms, more or less, and immunize ourselves against a few diseases. We can get from place to place with amazing rapidity, and see and talk around the world. We can explode molecules and theories with equal facility. But about all that any of it amounts to is that we are free to live bored and restless lives for a longer time, with greater efficiency, and over a wider area than ever before!

How the sect that calls itself Humanist has been able to build a religion out of its confidence in humanity, and in what humanity can do to make the world a better place, is more than I have ever been able to figure out. There simply is no mastery worth talking about in any of the realms that count! We have beautiful symbols, yes; towering notions of the higher life: and from generation to generation we continue to make a mess of them. There is the lady who carries a torch on that island in the harbor of New York and calls herself Liberty. She's lovely, as an ideal; but she presides today over as driven a people as any, driven by fear, by poverty, by wealth, by pleasure, the only redeeming feature of it all being that we can vote for the particular kind of vexation of spirit we like best, if we are willing to take the trouble! And there is that other lady called Justice, who is blindfolded and carries a sword and a pair of scales. Recently we blasphemed her fair name in the sovereign state of New Jersey by staging one of the coarsest shows of which a civilized country was ever guilty, and letting it pass for the Hauptmann trial. The verdict that was rendered was not properly subject to your scrutiny or to mine; but the commercialized horror of the crowds and the newspapers and the motion pictures and the radio were. But the great American public, far from raising a very hurricane of protest against all such wanton cheapness, shrugged its shoulders and went on grumbling about the much more important real estate situation! If we want to worry, why not worry about the right things?

These are only a few of the reasons I have—I could recite a score! —for submitting to you that humanity is still in a world that's too strong for it. Its attempts to get the upper hand have never yielded any very impressive results. Some hundred years back Horace Mann prophesied in Boston, with his accustomed eloquence, that crime would be wiped out, slowly but surely, with the increase in size and number of tax-supported schools; and slowly but surely his prophecy has been stultified by the facts. You should see how healthy the growth of prisons has been since we took over with more enthusiasm our responsibilities in the field of learning!

With still less likelihood of any success, we have of late begun again steadily to push forward our experiments in the way of peace by this fool's logic of preparedness, which consists in getting ready for war. Battleships shall be the pledge of our national security. We shall build them bigger, forever bigger, and sail the seven seas, until we bring home that dove with the olive-branch in her mouth!

No; some of us have conceived such a lack of confidence in humanity and in what it can do that we are willing at last to establish our religion, not on the faith that we have in the unfettered spirit of man, but precisely on the faith that we haven't: which indeed is what Jesus of Nazareth quite obviously did. "Without me," these were his words, "ye can do nothing!" And all the common sense of history is on his side! The world is too strong for us. It would be a great saving of time if we could start out with that, instead of winding up with it. We'd get a tremendous jump that way on this business of living!

But let's go on. Next, if we want to be consecutive in our thinking, and make a bit of progress toward this text, we ought to dismiss our futile attempts at power and look for a moment at the power of God. Wherever you come on it you will find it making itself felt through what passes with us for weakness! His ideas of strength seem to be altogether different from ours!

Here for instance is the world of Nature. What impresses us with the might that's there is the occasional outburst, the earthquake, the storm, that plays havoc with our little selves. Whittier writes of it in Snow-Bound:

> The shrieking of the mindless wind,
> The moaning tree-boughs swaying blind,
> And on the glass the unmeaning beat
> Of ghostly finger-tips of sleet.

If I may put it to you like this, what impresses God about it, I think, so that he might well smile in the sense of his own eternal adequacy, is the power within his world which is not of the earthquake or of the wind or of the fire, but of a likeness to some still, small voice,— holding silently the stars in their orbits for a child to lie awake and gurgle at; pressing up in blades of grass for cattle to tramp down, ripping it off in great mouthfulls and crunching it all night long in the meadow.

Power! We paint you a picture of the Pennsylvania's Red Arrow Express, or whatever it is, crossing the bridge near Harrisburg, with the wheels spinning, and the steam spitting from the cylinders, and the smoke billowing out from the funnel in black clouds. That's Power, say we! And God's symbols look so helpless: a midnight sky; the green carpet of the spring! Whose symbols are better?

I remember reading an account of how Mr. Einstein was talking one day about atomic energy. He said there was enough in a lump of coal the size of a pea to take the *Mauretania* across the Atlantic and back. A handful of snow would heat a large apartment house for a year. The pasteboard in a small railroad ticket would run a heavy passenger train several times around the globe. A teaspoonful of water would raise a load of a million tons to the top of a mountain six miles high. No doubt we should laugh out loud if some artist were to put these things on canvas and label them Power; but science wouldn't laugh! The only God she can guess at works that way!

Or take it of human life. That's more to the point. Here are Hitler and Mussolini, shall we say, both of them symbols of the world's growing hunger for a leadership that does things. We in America have our own heroes whose virtues we annually extol. It's quite right. And yet, somehow, I carry around a different notion of the way in which God commonly gets things done! He and James Abbott McNeill Whistler once painted the portrait of a mother, you remember it, sitting there in a long chair with her hands folded and her face and body resting toward the right. You never saw a figure of lonelier helplessness, crying out to every fibre of manhood in you for protection! And one says it in the same breath, you never saw a figure with a more appalling measure of all there is in human life that's strong: a patience, and a love, and a hope, that won't ever let go! We call it weakness, and for power prefer perhaps Peale's romantic portrait of Washington: God calls it strength, and keeps on sending people like many a man's mother into this work-a-day world of ours to hold it together!

All through the Book there he gets things done by an odd galaxy of men and women that never could have gone very far by themselves: an Abraham coming out of the East with wondering eyes; a Moses stammering his way through a wilderness; an Elijah pitted against a queen and a thousand priests; an Isaiah, a Jeremiah, standing solidly, if alone, in a nation's face; and at the end, a young Jew on a Roman cross! Was there ever such a token of utter weakness and abysmal rout given humanity as those two beams of wood with their quivering freight of a manhood not yet in its prime? It's the weakness that's the theme of the Book; yes, and of this whole symphony, in minor key, called human life—swelling to its climax on Calvary, there to be transmuted into the only pledge you and I have to cherish of God's resistless power to cleanse and hold and recreate the very stuff a soul is made of! Writes Browning, as he comes once more upon that eternal paradox of Majesty with nails in its hands and feet:

> I think this is the authentic sign and seal
> Of Godship, that it ever waxes glad,
> And more glad, until gladness blossoms, bursts
> Into a rage—a rage to suffer for mankind,
> And re-commence at sorrow.

Ah well, you say, what has it all to do with us? Just this: Christ, with the world still on his heart, isn't asking of us strength. That's something to get hold of in these days of ours when so clearly the world is too strong for us! Since the time when Israel sent out her spies from the wilderness, the call never has been for giants who could spread themselves around through the Promised Land with their thumbs in their armholes! But for a people yonder on the borders of Canaan, bewildered, in their own sight as grasshoppers, if only they will lift up the hands of faith without fear and go in to possess it!

Shall we set it down in plain words? What you and I can do will never amount to much; and nobody can say it with too great an emphasis: the best we have to offer is tainted with the poor self that offers it! But what God can do with the kind of love that refuses to have its feelings hurt; the patience that declines to quit; the hope that begs to be excused, please, from giving up: this is quite beyond your figuring! He can write a Bible with them, and redeem a world!

That's why there's no escape for any of us. It isn't quietism I'm suggesting. There's no getting away and hiding behind our inabilities; no hour in the day, no day in the week, when with a sigh of near-pious regret we may lay aside the dreams we have been cherishing because they are too hard now. For then and just there you meet this text striding down the middle of the road. "My strength is made perfect in weakness." There are no buts, and no ifs, and no althoughs. When the last stanchion has fallen down, and the stays have been chopped out from under you, when your confidence has been completely shattered, and you've conceived a thoroughgoing distrust of everything you've been counting on; when there's nothing left to get you through: then God's ready to start! It's there and just then you'll begin to feel the lift of everlasting arms!

Strong, upstanding, confident people may wriggle and squirm all they like; but there it is. Paul squirmed, too. Something he called a thorn stood there in the very sinews of his apostleship, humiliating him, insinuating its ugly self against all his plans, canceling his hopes one by one, or so it seemed to him, and it wouldn't budge. He tried to wriggle out into some measure of self-reliance three times by way of his prayer. He wanted a little bit of human wholeness under his feet to be a man on! "In God's name," he cried, "let me be free to run, free from this hounding infirmity that holds its nose at my heels!" And all he got on his lonely island of discontent was the hint and murmur of the sea, God's greatness around his incompleteness, round his restlessness God's rest! "It is enough that you have my grace." The word kept whispering itself down through the silence out of heaven; and it didn't seem right! He had preached to others about the weakness that was stronger than strength, and the foolish things that had been chosen to confound the wise; but it wasn't so easy to get hold of, now that his old winged sermon had come home to roost! It was like falling through endless space, getting such an answer as that, there in his closet, behind the closed door! Until the day he struck bottom! You've come up with it now; you've come up with the text! He knelt there, dazed suddenly at the distance he had fallen from his own esteem. But when he struggled up from his knees, it was GOD he had under his feet to be a man on!

"My strength is made perfect in weakness."

TROUBLE-BORN STARS

I therefore, the prisoner of the Lord. . . .
EPHESIANS iv:1

IT WAS one of the ways Paul had of making music out of discord. "I therefore, the prisoner of the Lord. . . ." As a matter of fact, he was a prisoner of Nero, chained by the ankle to a soldier; and no doubt he could have written a book about his experiences which the publishers would have been glad to get! But he was very modest about it, and quickly set it down, not as any extraordinary hardship, like a person looking for sympathy, but as part of that constant "pageant of triumph" into which he tells us God was always turning his life. "I therefore, the prisoner of the Lord. . . ." He was proud, really: proud to be in jail again; because it was for the "same old blessed reason"! And he wanted his friends to share, as well as they could at such a distance, the glory of it.

Besides, he had made good use of his time. With that soldier chained to him there, he was always sure of somebody to talk to about this Christ, "who dwelleth in me," he said. The guard's eyes must have opened pretty wide at that, and at some of the other things that were written down in letters to people who lived far away in Philippi, or farther still in Colossae or Ephesus. When the chains came off at night there was a good deal to tell the legionnaires about, at messtime, in the barrack rooms—with many a jest at first, no doubt; but gravely enough later on, as first one soldier and then another trudged back through the dusk after a shift with that strange fellow in chains who talked so incessantly and seemed so content. Until one day a letter went out carrying queer tidings, but true: "The name of Christ is known throughout the camp."

"I therefore, the prisoner of the Lord. . . ." You see what had happened. Paul had fallen on calamity, and whipped it into a blessing. He had turned a prison into a pulpit and a printing press for the kingdom of God. He had taken a peck of trouble in his hands and made a bushel of stars out of it, for brave spirits to hang up on dark nights.

Of course, with us, speaking of trouble is like speaking of opera-

143

tions: we've all got a story to tell. And frequently those of us who have never known what real trouble is, have the most to say! Little things seem to get under our skin and irritate us until we are broken out with them all over, like a rash: and we keep scratching them in public. We lose a watch or a pair of gloves, and can't comprehend why we have been singled out by a hostile destiny for such constant persecution! Most of our lesser misfortunes are our own fault; but we like to account for them by creeping in under the shadow of some mysterious adversity, and complaining that things are against us. We look downtrodden that way, and interesting, after the fashion of the early Christian martyrs. It's an odd, persistent notion this, that having the neighbors think our lot a hard one adds somehow to the zest of living. We lie in no bed of roses, and we want that distinctly understood. You have it easy, whoever you are, compared with us. And so, I dare say, nine-tenths of the gratitude we owe to God drops out of our lives by the back door of some imaginary hardship!

But there is real trouble in the world; and as often as not it tries bravely to wear a shining face. There are pain, and anxiety, and loss, and separation, and loneliness, and broken hopes, and the ashes of burnt-out fires. Only the heart of God, I suppose, could possibly bear the knowledge of that great sum total of human suffering and disappointment and sorrow which drags the weight of its feet along from dawn to dark all through the days. And usually it's quite shy. It doesn't say much. I wish it would say more, so that one man might be to another what Isaiah calls "an hiding place from the wind, and a covert from the tempest": how does it go?—"as rivers of water in a dry place, as the shadow of a great rock in a weary land." Too often it's just plain peevishness that's vocal, while the deeper anguish, though now and then to unburden itself would be half the cure, goes about in the dignity of silence. That's the type of trouble that I want to speak of: to the man or the woman who makes little or nothing of life's irritations; but like some timid wild thing that goes off into the woods with its fatal hurt to be alone, sits down with something that's beyond the reach of words. Such experiences come to all of us sooner or later, and we move into dark places which no one can share with us. What then?

Well, the first thing, it seems to me, is to remember that the true bearing and significance of every condition lie in the issue of it.

All the genuine trouble there is in the world is of itself a problem that leaps right in the face of a good God, and there's no use trying to deny it. Either he isn't almighty, or he isn't good: many a rebellious mood feels that way about it. Job looked at his own life, and got off on that foot more than once. Ecclesiastes looked at the life around him, and was inclined to draw the same conclusion. So were half a dozen other frank and gallant souls here in the Book, who were bent on being outspoken with God, not behind his back, but before his very throne! There is a problem there.

And it isn't of very much use trying to explain it, either. It just wearies a man who has the hurt in his eyes to keep offering him small doses of "proverbial philosophy or conventional religion," riddling him with a maxim-gun, as someone has put it. The "comfort of a trite theology" is cruel comfort, talking about everything's being for the best, and some day we'll understand!

Let's be honest, anyway, and if we don't quite get the drift of God's dealing, why then at least grapple this one solid, reliable fact: that what matters ultimately is not so much the trouble as what comes of it. That's as clear as the multiplication table. Some people get nothing but sourness and cynicism out of it: they want to consign life itself to hell, and all human hopes with it. But while that's one possible up-shot, it isn't inevitable. Job will show you how far over on the other side of things from bitterness a soul can come, on its way out of trouble: it can come straight up before the bewildering majesty of God and worship there, with an awe that lays its hand over its mouth, and a heart that goes on whispering to itself, "Though he slay me, yet will I trust him!"

Or take Ecclesiastes. He had to fight through difficult times, with mobs in the street, and an "unscrupulous and suspicious tyrant" on the throne. Besides, he had had a bad attack of temperament for many years, and was thoroughly depressed. So he begins with a weary refrain, full of despondent scepticism: "Vanity of vanities, all is vanity!" He moves on through a thousand "wild and whirling words," going round the circle of life; until at last he—or perhaps some later and adventurous soul—seems to come back to the place from which he started. But this time whoever it is comes as a victor, and his cry of "Vanity, vanity!" has in it now the faith he has won; turning its back on all there is of emptiness, which is a being without God in the world, and singing its stately hymn alone, with the wisdom which has followed on the heels of a long journey: "Remember now thy Creator in the days of thy youth."

Oh yes; you can come out of the hot furnace of trouble two ways: if you let it consume you quite, you come out a cinder; but there is a kind of metal which refuses to be consumed, and comes out a star. "I therefore, the prisoner of the Lord. . . ." There are people who fall on calamity and whip it into a blessing; and you've got to count them in when you sit down to read the riddle of life! Pain, anxiety, loss, separation, loneliness—none of it stands by itself: there's always what comes of it. And it does seem that a man can shape that as he will! "Out of prison he cometh to reign." So wrote this wise old preacher, Ecclesiastes; and Joseph did it, and Paul did it, and poor John Bunyan did it!

Let's write down in our minds, then, just three brief words of counsel. One of them is simply this: Push on! If you are ever puzzled by any of these dark places in human experience—as no doubt some day you will be, when your own foot slips into them—don't stand there dazed and uncertain, wondering if God loves you. Understanding may not be in your power, but obedience is: and when you go on about his will, you're at peace. That much is sure, and lying there for anybody to pick up and make his own! It isn't a terminus, this ill-fortune of yours, whatever it is: it's a thoroughfare; and hard as the going may be, there will come a dawn or a sunset when you'll be through it. All that's left of it then will be written here in your soul. Pray God it may not be bitterness, but the beauty that's waiting for folk who go on! Perhaps as you look back in that hour you may even wonder that it ever seemed dark!

Dr. Hutton once wrote a little essay on what he called "The Dark Mile." It was the name given a short stretch of road between two lakes in Scotland. He and his American friend had long planned to walk it together, though more than a little afraid of its gloomy canyons, and noisy torrents, and over-hung rocks. One day, with a forced jauntiness, comforting themselves with a sort of strained laughter, they started out. And as they went they began talking eagerly back and forth of distant hopes and fond recollections, forgetful for a while of their fears, stopping only for a moment to look at the "little clouds lying about the fields of heaven like sheep," and at a lark that sprang singing out of the hedge. Almost before they knew it, they stood on the shores of Loch Lochy, gazing at one another in a kind of bewilderment. "Let me see that map!" said the American; and after looking at it intently for a bit, he lifted his head. "What a world!" And he wiped his brow. "Do you know— that was the Dark Mile, and we never even saw it! We were standing in the heart of it just there in yon canyon where the lark rose!" Many a soul that hasn't stopped to brood, but has pushed on, can bear that witness about dark miles!

"I therefore, the prisoner of the Lord. . . ." He had made up his mind to one thing: he wouldn't stop in that jail, though he had to stay there! "And ever, as the day wore on, the trouble grew; wherefrom he guessed there would be born a star!"

The second word that ought to be spoken to a man who is having what seems to him more than his share, pressed together and running over, of the world's woe, has been phrased very quaintly by a Japanese: "When I dig another out of trouble," so his discovery runs, "the hole from which I lift him is the place where I bury my own!" And that, I think, is the eternal mystery of the cross, standing at the very center of human life. It was all because Christ was forever bearing other men's loads, that the weight of his own grew nothing! He stood there one day, looking around the circle of the crowd, saying to them with such earnestness, "My yoke is easy, and my burden is light." Your eye wanders off to Calvary, and the forsaken-ness of that cry in the dark, and you shake your head: No, Christ; no! We can't get under that. You're asking too much! But he still gazes at you, wondering that you don't understand. Other men's loads make the burden light! Slowly he swings off across the hills into Eternity, still wondering; with that parting gesture of his, and the very word he used as a schoolboy at Nazareth, giving good-by to his friends: "Shalom!" It was like the "So long" that we call sometimes across the widening spaces between us. Very like. "Not as the world gives it, do I say unto you Shalom. Peace." Across the hills, with your burden and mine; that's why there was peace in his soul to give away, above the cross, and on it, and beneath it, and all around.

Dostoievsky, a prisoner in Siberia, once talked as he walked with little Sonia. And "when he might, by all the obvious rules, have belched forth smoke and flames in detestation of life's brutalities, he would speak only, with a terrible and persistent gentleness, of how we all need to be kind to one another, seeing what sorrows are apt to come!"

So, too, with Paul.

"I therefore, the prisoner of the Lord. . . ." He wasn't feeling his feelings, and letting the world drag on without any help from him. "The God of all comfort," he wrote to the Corinthians, "who comforteth us in all our afflictions, that we may be able to comfort them that are in any affliction, through the comfort wherewith we ourselves are comforted of God." It's under other men's loads that the weight of our own grows nothing!

Finally, as we push on, digging as many as we can out of trouble on the way, to keep the doors and windows of our lives open upon God! That's all then that remains to be said. I often wonder why it is that people so frequently shut themselves away from the church, sometimes even from prayer, when they come upon days of gloom and heavy weather. It isn't as though this God, who asks us to take him into our confidence, were a stranger to grief.

> Hath he marks to lead me to him,
>   If he be my Guide?
> In his feet and hands are wound-prints,
>   And his side!

He doesn't come to us without the seal and evidence of the road he has traveled, so that none can ever travel any so bitter! To keep our lives open to him. It's only fair! Here is one who is doing it. "I am only fifty-five," she writes to me, "but my body feels eighty. So much to be done, and so little strength for the doing. Thursday is my day at the specialist's, and on Friday the sky often seems very dark, and Christ far away. I am in the house alone all through the week, from six in the morning until nine at night. But whenever I read something from the New Testament I seem to get back my courage. Today," she adds, in her homely way, "I canned twelve quarts of tomatoes. That makes fifty-nine for me in all. Your work and mine are different, but I certainly will try to believe that I have a part in God's plan, and I will try to fill it as best I can. I must lie on my bed now and rest." She, too, could rebel, or break down, or fold her hands, and let things go; but here is her gallant little note, not knowing how the journey will end, just sure that it's hers to hold on; with a soul that has its windows open on God!

That's how stars are born!

It's odd how many people lift their faces to them as they shine through the night! This Paul is one. "I therefore, the prisoner of the Lord, . . ." turning a prison into a pulpit like that, and making a cold, stone bench into a printing press for the kingdom of God!

AS A MATTER OF FACT—

THE BOOK OF THE AGES

For whatsoever things were written aforetime were
written for our learning, that we through patience and
comfort of the Scriptures might have hope.

Romans xv:4

O R ACCORDING to Dr. Moffatt, ". . . Such words were written of old for our instruction, that by remaining steadfast and drawing encouragement from the Scriptures we may cherish hope."

That would seem to be quite enough to make the Bible attractive: instruction, steadfastness, encouragement, hope. It has recently been found necessary, however, to add other features. "Something new!" runs the advertisement. "Rainbow Bibles. The Book of Books in color. Bibles that are not solemn or forbidding but beautiful and appealing. Bibles that will be read so much more often because of their attractiveness. Three gorgeous colors, green cloth, blue leather, purple morocco, with gold edges." Somehow it strikes me with a kind of sardonic humor. We shall soon be announcing for physicians a new edition of all the standard textbooks on therapeutics rendered more readable in antique red, and for lawyers a Blackstone they will love to handle with a cover by Howard Chandler Christy! It's a cheap if rather pathetic attempt to bolster the sales of a Book which though never more useful than today was perhaps never less used, never more widely sold and never more consistently unread. We seem to think that somehow what can be retained from the heritage of our training in the schools of the church and from the weekly service of worship is quite enough: the memory of disjointed stories, and the familiar ring of a hundred gracious promises and solemn precepts. They are all like the fragments of half-forgotten scenes, little wisps of conversation, recurring now and then from a shadowy past; and around them have been built at odd times grotesque ideas of duty, shapeless romance, queer prejudices, fond expectation, bitter disappointment.

That there is still in it for us, like the strong flowing of a current, "instruction, steadfastness, encouragement, hope"—this hardly occurs to us now. Besides, ours is rather a taste for the transient, and we trust the flavor will be high enough to touch up our jaded palates. It's decidedly the day for Book-of-the-Month Clubs—almost any book will do if the printer's ink isn't dry. And we know what they are like, many of them, before we read them. Glance over the brief reviews that are appearing in every magazine as suggestions for your shopping. "The story of a twice-married lady and the five days she wavered between the husband who had loved her not wisely and the one who had loved her too well." Or this: "A tire exploded. His friends bent over him. He was dead. Before he saw them again he stood at a gate and heard the amazing dictum that scared him back to life, knew that he must return to cheat a partner and"—but we'd better cancel the rest of his activities! Life does look just now as if it might have been built on some such foundation!

And so it has occurred to me that in "the universal flux" of modern America a "Book-of-the-Ages Club" would be infinitely more to the point. We have been running around long enough trying by way of football games and moving pictures to escape from the tension under which we are living. We have lavished dimes and quarters on newsstands in our effort to achieve a little relaxation. And everywhere, on the stage and in the novel, in dailies, weeklies, monthlies, we are brought face to face, cynically, with the same worthless aspects of human life: you may take your choice of them between killing and stealing and adultery, with a few complexes thrown in. And we call that our recreation! If anybody thinks it's a reasonable program let him go ahead with it. Those of us who have a few misgivings may stop and think it over.

What we really need is some "point of permanence in all this vast drifting of the cosmic weather." We need something that's like a rock under our feet, and a clean wind through our souls. We need some strong conviction that life is meaningful, and not just a purposeless and unclean microbe down here on "the epidermis of a midget." We need a thorough-going self-respect, and some purifying, enabling sense of God. Give this to us, give it to us every day that we live, and a good deal that we call relaxation will begin to slough off without being missed. It isn't so much our moods that need to be lightened by the four Marx brothers, or our minds that need to be refreshed by Mr. John Erskine or Mr. van Dine, or our muscles that need to be set up with golf clubs. There is, if you please, a kind of re-creation which goes deeper than any of that: and we leave it untried until we get into some kind of genuine difficulty!

"Since childhood," reads another kind of advertisement entirely, "we have heard what a great Book the Bible is. We accept that as a fact, and go along for years nodding our heads and saying 'yes.' Once in a while, or maybe oftener, we read a passage or two. Then something happens. Things go wrong, troubles begin to pile up, we don't know what to do. We try this and that and all the time there on the table lies the Bible tight shut. Now and then some man or woman facing defeat sits down with it and suddenly finds it talking like a friend, encouraging, guiding. With wide eyes and joy in his heart he discovers why it is called the Book of Books; not for its poetry, not for its history, but for the help it gives. It's something you can't realize until it happens to you. But when it does you always remember it."

The suggestion I'm trying to make is that you don't have to wait until you suffer a nervous breakdown before you begin to indulge in the right sort of relaxation, nor put off your discovery of the Book until you "face defeat"! It will never yield the best it has on any such terms. There is a kind of deep-sea diving that can be done only in quiet waters. Nor am I commending it to you simply because "it's good for you." There's no magic efficacy about it as there seems to be about all particularly bad-tasting medicine, which needs only that you should shut your eyes and take your daily dose. It isn't one of those things that come under the category of duty. I know how thoroughly this age resents that word; and I resent it, too, when you begin to apply it to religion! When you discharge your duty you're done with it, and God, with all he has to be and say, will not be treated so! I tell you, it's life that's in this Book; don't chatter to me about duty: it's all right in its place, but this isn't its place! It isn't your duty to live: it's a chance you have. It's a door standing wide open into a vast room of undiscovered wealth. It's the beckoning coast of a strange continent with nameless rivers and mountains all unexplored. No, it isn't "good for you," nothing so tame as that. It's a horizon, it's a vista, it's a landscape. I don't care what you call it, only let your word be round as God, and long as life, and wide as love; then gird yourself when you enter on it and catch your breath! That's the Bible! And the issue of it is a new world!

Let's see if you can make a proper approach to it. Most of us come with our mouths full of questions as a woman's occasionally used to be of hairpins, so that every time we open them a question falls out! Is the Bible true? What about the Virgin Birth? Who wrote the fourth gospel? Do you believe in miracles? Is the Sermon on the Mount really practical? A friend of mine once underlined all these matters in red ink, and kept up an active search for others that he couldn't believe! Strangely enough, when it came to food his whole method seemed to change: he never was known to spend all his time asking questions at a banquet; he looked around carefully for nourishment! Such inconsistent dealing isn't distinguished for its moral earnestness or its intellectual integrity. It's just another indication that the Bible is demonstrably more reliable than the people who try to discredit it. Let any man come to this Book for the wealth it has to give him; let him sit down to it reverently, for all that it has wrought in the world; let him read it as if it were the record of God's progressive revelation of himself in life; let him quietly brood again and again over its familiar stories, trace the growth of its ideas, as step by step they learn to do their towering—God and the soul, sin and death, life and immortality—let him set out for himself down that pilgrim way, and he'll soon have done with controversy, and come to discovery! Don't tell me you haven't time. You've time to live!

And this is what he'll find. It's here in the text, and it's enough! "Such words were written of old for our instruction, that by remaining steadfast and drawing encouragement from the scriptures we may cherish hope." Instruction that will render us *steadfast*. That's the first great word, and I want you to look at it. The Greek of it means to stay right on under a load no matter how heavy it becomes: not to fall down, and not to slide out. Is that by any chance what you need? I've seen many an athlete do it— standing there while one by one his friends built themselves into a human pyramid, from his waist far above his head, and he stood there smiling! I saw a man with graying hair do it, as he lost his wife, a daughter, a son, and still another; and he came on smiling! Paul did it when life piled up on him; and he said the secret was in the Book! He ought to know. Doesn't it lie in just this: the long panorama of heroic life these pages unfold before you, men with burdens on top of burdens, and on their faces peace, like the peace of God? That, says the Bible, is what life can be, when on it is laid the hand of its Creator: Moses, Elijah, Isaiah, and a Man there with a cross, saying "Peace be unto you." God wants something carried, and you don't like it? Is that it? And page by page he whispers, "It's the way to peace! Too heavy for you, is it?" And through the turning leaves a still voice: "Not too heavy for you—and me! Steadfast!" And you stand there—smiling! It's the message of the Book!

"Remaining steadfast and drawing *encouragement* from the Scriptures." That's the second great word. Look at it. It means the calling of another to one's side for counsel and companionship and cheer. Who that other is, is no secret in the Book! He journeyed with Abraham out of Ur of the Chaldees, and with Joseph when they sold him a slave into Egypt. Back again when the years were gone, dry-shod through the sea: "Speak unto the children of Israel, that they go forward!" A cloud and a fire in the desert; like the sun standing still to Joshua, in the valley of Ajalon; to David, a rustling in the tops of the mulberry trees; a whisper to Samuel in the night; to the prophet, a ringing charge, "Son of Man, stand up!" And then on the lake, a vision to twelve men rowing: "It is I; be not afraid!" Westward to Greece and Rome with Paul, and to John on Patmos, as the surf rolled in, one "who was dead and is alive forevermore!" Like Shakespeare's Henry—that "little touch of Henry in the dark." Has your world tumbled in? Have you lost your poise? With that love at the heart of the universe, and the arm there which wrought it all! "Be of good courage! Before the day was, I am. No man can pluck thee out of my hand. I will work, and who shall turn it back?" It's the message of the Book! And you there alone?

"By remaining steadfast and drawing encouragement from the Scriptures we may cherish *hope*." Is that anything to you? Hope! With your life what it is? That year by year it may grow clean and strong before the face of him, all the wrong of it straight forgiven, no radiant thing beyond your reach? Hope! In my book of synonyms they say it's just another word for "illusion," for "mirage" and "will-o'-the-wisp." Stand here through the ages with this God, in the presence of this Christ, and tell me how it seems! With Matthew there an evangelist, and Mary of Magdala all in white, and that mighty Augustine, and dear St. Francis, and stalwart Luther, and poor John Bunyan in Bedford jail! I've come clear out of the covers of the Bible and Christ has come, too, with the hope men call a fable!

Back in the days of Israel when all the people of the northern Kingdom had fallen away into idolatry, there lived a man whose name was Hosea. Life had dealt but poorly with him. With exquisite tenderness he had redeemed his faithless wife from her lovers "for the price of a slave" and "tried to win her back to purity and love by gentle restraint." But in it all, wistfully he saw the loving kindness of God toward his faithless nation, and looking out over a landscape of bitterness, he mused like that Eternal Lover. "Behold, I will woo her, and bring her into the wilderness, and speak to her heart. I will give her back her vineyards, and the valley of troubling for a door of hope." "It's the message of the Book!" "The valley of troubling"—have you ever been there?—"for a door of hope!"

In these days of books by the month, my friends ask me if I'm "keeping up in my reading." I wonder if they mean "keeping *up*!" It isn't difficult to keep *up*—with God!

THE RISK OF PRAYER

*The end of all things is at hand: be ye therefore sober,
and watch unto prayer.*

I PETER iv:7

I WONDER if you sense the true spirit of that. Dr. Moffatt has
caught it better I think in his translation: "Now the end of
all is near. Steady then, keep cool and pray." The world was on the
verge of catastrophe. Peter was sure of it. Judgment was coming.
A man must stand steadily on his feet. He mustn't lose control of
himself and become hysterical. He must be cool, like a sentinel
in the face of danger. And he must pray.

What I want you to notice is that prayer in the mind of Peter
has got itself associated with peril; not as a refuge, but as part
of the risk. If you'll read the rest of the chapter you'll see. He tells
these scattered Christians they have to be ready to suffer. They
are going to be reviled and persecuted in the very teeth of their
love. And prayer isn't going to keep them from it. In fact, quite
the contrary: every time they pray they are sure to increase the
hazards. Because the world they live in frankly doesn't like the
praying sort. It didn't like Christ before them. It made life as hard
as it could for him, and death, too. They need not hope to be
any exception to the rule. Prayer would get them right straight
into trouble. They'd have to hold fast, and not lose their heads.
This was no sweet-smelling ointment, no salve for sore consciences,
no pillow for infirm wills, no picnic for anybody—this getting down
on one's knees, or lifting up one's arms to heaven, and really
praying! It was an appalling risk!

Suppose we try to adjust ourselves today to his way of thinking.
It's far nearer the truth than our own. Of that I'm convinced. Most
of our praying is made up of selfish petition, the asking for things
that will make life a little more safe and comfortable and to our
liking. I have read of how Jules Romain, as congregations bowed
their heads in church, tried to feel around in the air for the things
they were saying, climbing up to God like blue smoke from the
soul's hearth. Here they were as he fancied them:

O God in heaven, vouchsafe to cure my leg!—
    to fill my shop with customers.
Help me to find out if my servant John
Is robbing me! O God, cure my sore eyes!
Save me, O God, from being drunk so often!
Lord, let my son pass his examination!
Help me to make her fall in love with me!
My God, if only I could get some work!
My husband makes a martyr of me. Let me die!

It's like the crowd of cripples on the porch at the pool of Bethesda, waiting around for the water to bubble: all invalids! And Peter wants us to believe that prayer is a sort of sentry-business in the soul of a man who's headed for trouble, and absurdly happy! What a chasm! God help us for a while. We must try to bridge it! We have to get over from our way of thinking to his.

Prayer is a lifetime—a year, a month, a week, a day—an hour, a moment—of vital contact between the soul and God. I am not saying that it isn't petition. One recent author suggests that we stop using it that way entirely. I don't see how we can hold on to the Lord's Prayer if we do! That's full of petition from beginning to end. But it isn't selfish petition, any of it. It doesn't want to get off or be spared anything. It isn't trying to hobble around sore legs, and empty shops, and weak eyes, and unemployment, on a pair of heaven-sent crutches! This prayer is too proud and gallant to pray like that! I saw quoted the other day an incident from A. S. M. Hutchinson's "The Uncertain Trumpet." Jim Heritage had gone over the side of the yacht in the night after his friend Bill who couldn't swim. The yacht couldn't find them as they clung exhausted to the rim of a buoy marking the channel, and they watched it leave, its lights blinking farther and farther away through the dark. They knew they couldn't hang on much longer. "I guess we're booked through this time," said Jim; "no return tickets." Then a silence. "Pretty rotten, wouldn't you say," asked the other after a few moments, "to start praying, now we're up against it?" "Yes, Bill, pretty rotten," said Jim; "best go through as we have run." And first one and then the other slipped off into the darkness. "Our Father Who art in heaven." Petition? Yes! It's full of it. But they are brave petitions. They hold up their heads.

They wouldn't stoop to whine, and dodge, and fend off, and let their teeth chatter with a beggar's fear! They march right along from a name into a kingdom, with a will, through bread, and trespasses, and temptation, and evil, to power and glory forever and ever. Amen!

A day, an hour, a moment of vital contact between the soul and God. I am not saying that prayer isn't petition, and I am not saying that prayer isn't communion. It is. As a man sits by the hearth in fellowship with his friend, never thinking to make life smoother by it, catching the inspiration of that other's presence, sharing the vision of those other eyes, and then goes out into the busy world with peace again: so may a man before the fire sit with God! "Whether thou comest in sunshine or in rain," cries George Matheson, "I would take thee into my heart. Thou art thyself more than the sunshine. Thou art thyself compensation for the rain. It is thee, not thy gifts I crave." And yet, what would happen if we really found him there, on the hearth, in front of the fire? Haven't we sentimentalized this word communion until it sounds like a dressing gown, and slippers, and a long sigh of content? Isn't it that we've forgotten how disturbing a person God is to meet? In the Old Testament they were quite sure it would be dreadful, and would mean death. Where did we ever get the idea that a little communion with God before retiring would top things off nicely?

It's like the advertisement which I understand they give you these days at the foot of Mt. Blanc. There was a time, so I read, when no one even thought of attempting the climb. It was far too dangerous. After a while it became a still difficult, but possible feat for the hardiest of mountaineers. Now with all our modern conveniences, it's advertised as "an easy day for a lady." Communion with God, and we walk off into it as though it couldn't be anything but a sweet haven of rest! George Matheson didn't! He knew! Read his hymn about the love that would not let him go, and how he had to give it back the life he owed, and the flickering torch he carried, and how he saw there the cross, and wouldn't ask to flee from it. When those two met, God and George Matheson, it was no quiet evening by the fire! There were "ocean depths" and "sunshine's blaze" and "blossoms red!" A man would do well to be staggered by it!

A day, an hour, a moment of vital contact between the soul and God. If that should ever really happen to you, let me tell you what you'd risk.

First of all you'd risk seeing yourself as you are! I wonder how many of us could stand that with a balanced mind. But Christ will show you yourself, surely he will: you must risk that when you pray!

Chalmers, in his book "The Commonplace Prodigal,"[1] quotes a poem from Studdert-Kennedy's "Sorrows of God." A cockney soldier after church has had a dream.

> I seemed to stand alone, beside
>   A solemn kind o' sea.
> Its waves they got in my inside,
>   And touched my memory.
> And day by day, and year by year,
>   My life came back to me.

He saw just what he was, and what he'd had a chance to be: the good he might have done, but hadn't stopped to do. And in that agony of soul he turned and found a figure standing beside him.

> All eyes was in 'is eyes—all eyes,
>   My wife's and a million more;
> And once I thought as those two eyes
>   Were the eyes of the London whore.
> And they was sad—my Gawd, 'ow sad,
>   Wiv tears that seemed to shine,
> And quivering bright wi' the speech o' light
>   They said, "'Er soul was mine."

It's in this setting that the word comes which is the title of the poem:

> And then at last 'e said one word,
>   'E said just one word—"Well?"
> And then I said in a funny voice,
>   "Please, sir, can I go to 'ell?"
> And 'e stood there and looked at me,
>   And 'e kind o' seemed to grow,

---

[1] To which I would acknowledge my debt here!

Till 'e shone like the sun above my 'ead,
  And then 'e answered, "No,
You can't; that 'ell is for the blind
  And not for those that see.
You know that you 'ave earned it, lad,
  So you must follow me.
Follow me on by the paths o' pain,
  Seeking what you 'ave seen,
Until at last you can build the 'Is'
  Wi' the brick o' the 'Might 'ave been.'"
That's what 'e said, as I'm alive,
  And that there dream was true.
But what 'e meant—I don't quite know;
  Though I know what I has to do.
I's got to follow what I's seen,
  Till this old carcase dies;
For I daren't face in the land o' grace
  The sorrow o' those eyes.
There ain't no throne, and there ain't no books,
  It's 'im you've got to see,
It's 'im, just 'im, that is the judge
  O' blokes like you and me.
And, boys, I'd sooner frizzle up
  I' the flames of a burning 'ell,
Than stand and look into 'is face,
  And 'ear 'is voice say—"Well?"

You've got to risk seeing yourself when you pray.

And you've got to risk growing more like Jesus of Nazareth; because that's bound to happen when prayer assumes the stature of reality in your life. And there's no use being sentimental about that. We used to have a hymn when I was a boy that everybody in Sunday school would sing with peculiar fervor; and, I have no doubt, with a great deal of genuine aspiration in their hearts. It began, "I want to be more like Jesus, and follow him day by day." Those words would have died on ninety-nine tongues out of every hundred if we had even for a moment thought of what they meant! Being like Jesus in a world like this isn't a prospect to be viewed with composure, from in front of a lovely altar, on comfortable seats! The apostles could tell you. It may be you have already given it up as impossible, and find now for your own failure a sort of strange compensation in idealizing what you can't attain! I think perhaps that has happened to a good many of us. We believe in love and unselfishness and sacrifice, in justice and mercy and peace; we salute them, one by one. We warm to the very thought of them. We do our obeisance to them, in the carpenter of Galilee: and somehow that gives us the feeling of having accomplished something! We don't really expect to take down such shining robes and put them on; but we admire them, and think it would be a good thing if people would wear them! Let's keep looking at them, anyhow; there's a certain amount of satisfaction in that!

But on the day that prayer becomes for you more than a pious exercise, more than a routine ordering of words you think God will like, on that day you'll have to risk wearing those robes yourself: loving in a world that wounds love, being unselfish in a world that takes advantage of unselfishness, saving in a world that crucifies Saviours! It won't matter how you fare. They'll jail you for not fighting, they'll cheat you for being honest, they'll hurt your feelings for showing yourself affectionate; but make no mistake about it: that's what you'll have to risk when you pray! Because, you see, God may answer your prayer and make you more like Jesus!

And you have to risk seeing that God's will instead of your own is done in and through your life. Think that over carefully. The will of God is the growth of your soul. There is much that stands in the way of it: there are desires whose noisy clamor you want to satisfy, sometimes you don't care much how you do it; there is the longing to possess, there are ambitions to be called this or hailed as something else. I don't know what stands in the way. You know, I'm sure of that. How about the kind of praying that means letting them go? The will of God is human brotherhood. How about the kind of praying that drops your prejudices, one after the other? Race, and social distinction, pride, and sensitiveness, and shyness, everything that walls you in from others and cuts you off? The will of God is economic justice, righteousness, the other fellow's chance to live. Is that one of your passions too? This new earth that's in his mind, with all that it's going to cost? Have you ever seen it? Do you think we need it? Is there anything you would withhold, anything you would put before your vision of the kingdom of God in the world? I'm not just talking. I'm telling you the risks you run, as your soul stands naked and alone in the presence of God! "Thy will be done!" And I'm not only going to get myself out of the way, Lord Jesus! Here are a mind and a heart you can count on, hands and feet. The preacher said yesterday, last week, last month, that it might cost—everything! All right! It's on the counter, and I'm glad to pay it over—because you see, I mean it—Thy will be done!

Prayer! God knows it's not a refuge! It strips you and leaves you bare to the sorrows of God! But let us pray!

I PRAYED—BUT . . .

For this thing I besought the Love . . .
II CORINTHIANS xii:8

PAUL gives us only one mention of the thorn that was in his flesh. He isn't the kind of person that would talk about it very much. He doesn't seem to be so intent as some of us are on having all his friends thoroughly acquainted with the handicap under which he's working. There are people, you know, who will deliberately turn the conversation into that channel on the slightest provocation: "Speaking of operations," or "talking of specialists" —and they're off! Queerly enough, it's a malady that seems to fasten especially and very grimly on the righteous: nobody can possibly know how righteous they are unless they give some publicity to the obstacles they have to overcome in the way of headaches and indigestion!—But Paul isn't of their tribe. This is no excuse he's making. The manner of the life he has lived, as he sets it down in his record, doesn't call for any excuse. Oddly he is rather boasting than complaining; boasting of a prayer he'd offered, and the strange issue of it: "I was given a thorn in the flesh; three times over I prayed the Lord to make it leave me, but He told me, 'It is enough for you to have my grace.'" It was a prayer that seemed quite futile—earnest prayer, prayer straight from the heart of triumphant faith, the prayer of a man whose body and soul with all his ways and will were God's; prayer that was like pleading three times repeated; prayer that had for its aim not any selfish relief but better equipment for a faster race and a harder fight and a greater triumph. And there were the words of Jesus standing up all round that prayer like guarantors: "Whatsoever ye shall ask in my name, He will give it you." "Ask and ye shall receive." "Seek and ye shall find." "To him that knocketh it shall be opened." It was stamped, and endorsed, and underwritten. And this was the fruit of it—or so it seemed: "I prayed—but . . . !" Matters didn't turn out in accordance with his prayer—that's all!

Suppose we write the rest of his biography in the fashion of our twentieth century Christianity. After these things Paul began to lose interest, and fell away from the church. His faith in human nature had been considerably shaken. It seemed as if he had met with nothing but opposition from start to finish. People who had been Christians longer than he, had put obstacles in his way. He was an outcast from among his own race. Uproars had broken out wherever he went. They had stoned him and mocked him. It hadn't been very encouraging. And there was the thorn. It was there to stay. Prayer didn't budge it. So he began to read some books on prayer. It didn't seem to work. Perhaps he could get along just as well without it. Why not? And he went back to his trade, and made tents. He amassed quite a fortune, for those days—before he died. The years grew very tranquil and undisturbed in their slow and equal pace from day to day. It was a great relief to him, except that he was never quite happy.

And there was the thorn. Among his last words there was something about having done a great deal better if it hadn't been for that thorn. He was buried in the presence of a few Greek merchants, friends of his, and when they read his will it was found that he had left all his money to be divided equally between the School of Philosophy at Tarsus and the altar-cult in Athens dedicated to The Unknown God.

Now go back and see how God finished the story. "I prayed three times over—but . . ." "It is enough for you to have my grace." Somebody else was to have his way, and this was the course of it: There was a long journey back to Jerusalem. It was a sad leave-taking there at Miletus: "I know," said he to his friends, "that ye shall see my face no more. . . . And when he had thus spoken, he kneeled down and prayed with them all." It was strange for one who had found nothing in prayer! From Tyre many disciples brought him on his way, with their wives and children, until he was well out of the city: and they kneeled down with him on the shore and prayed. Nothing in prayer! Strange. In Caesarea they besought him not to go on, and he answered, "I am ready not to be bound only, but to die at Jerusalem for the Name of the Lord Jesus." Nothing in prayer? How they sent him back after his appeal to Caesar, you know—and how shipwrecked he came a prisoner to Rome. That's the story, except for his martyrdom, and a few things he wrote from his prison: "I bow my knees unto the Father of our Lord Jesus Christ that He would grant you to be strengthened by

His spirit"— . . . "Who is able to do exceeding abundantly above all that we ask or think" . . . "In every prayer of mine making request with joy." . . . But Paul, there is nothing in prayer! "My God shall supply your need," Who "stood with me and strengthened me . . . and will preserve me unto His heavenly Kingdom: to Whom be glory for ever and ever. Amen." And there to gainsay him were still the thorn and the prayer, "Three times over I prayed, but . . ."

Against the background of such a life you will understand me when I say that I am particularly interested in that "but." Again and again it has slipped into your life and mine: we too have prayed—but . . . And then gradually it begins to dawn on me as I read: of all the places where men have ever written that word, in this place at least there is not even the shadow of disappointment in it. Paul's face didn't fall when he set it down; he caught his breath! It's time to catch your breath, and miss a heart-beat or two, when God answers the prayer you make with "No—but . . ." It's just his way of saying that he's going to take it over! Going to stride beyond your little horizons as though they didn't exist, and write such a record of fulfillment as you've never dreamed of! These poor tragic loves of ours down here go about for one another so pathetically among their treasures, pick one at last that's all wrong, and hold it out with a proud and smiling face: and that Love moves down out of the past and future to find God's Best when a human soul is on its knees! We take his will up in our hands and look at it, and then connect it with Gethsemane, and cups that are bitter to drink. "Thy will be done." There is that about it which makes us think of broken plans, and blind alleys from which there is no escape, and graves being filled with heavy, falling earth—as if all our dear hopes had been taken captive by it—by a sad, mysterious purpose, and made to surrender their short, bright lives in pitiful submission. And all the while we ought to be bearing ourselves, not with folded hands and mournful mien, but like a jubilant host before it, with a faith that springs

"Like the eagle's, who soars to meet the sun,
    And cries exulting unto Thee, Lord God, Thy will be done!"

"I prayed—but . . ." It's not the gesture of a bowed head; it's the gesture of a lighted lamp, and a man that's girding his loins to run a race that God has set before him, with goals it takes God to imagine!

And so I ask you to bring your hopes here, today, and tomorrow too, and all the days; just to this place where Paul knelt and prayed, and out of the silent, lonely void came a voice whispering in his soul, "My grace." Don't come hugging something close to your heart, and crying with a snarl, "It is this I must have—my way—my will—this, and this only." Your trinket against God's wealth! One random little gleaning, against the harvest! How blind we are! When out of our prayers—let them be poor and twisted—if only they are humble and sincere—when out of them this knowledge is to be had: that we are never, never alone; that on the road through the dark is the cheer of a lantern swinging, and the way we are taking is God's way, bigger than we've prayed, better than we've hoped, higher than we've dreamed.

No shabbiest prodigal of us all slouching through life but he misses us, and cannot forget, steals often to the door, gazes up and down, watching and hoping against hope; and then one day runs with out-stretched arms, "My son, my son!" "I prayed—I prayed him to make me as one of his hired servants, but . . ." "My son, my son!" That's God's way of answering prayer! And ever since, there have been men who have ventured to test it, and know now it is true! I met one of them one night. He drove me twenty-six miles by moonlight across the mountains to catch a train. And there over the steady hum of the motor he told me the story of his life. Until a few years ago it had run smoothly; and suddenly it launched out into deep and troubled waters. There were three deaths in his family, one on the heels of another; and "he had prayed—but . . ." I had been preaching that evening on the cross of Jesus, and there was a long silence between us. At last he said, "I know Him. It's a lonely road," and he looked out across the barren mountains; "I could not travel it alone."

Will you bring them all here, your prayers, where Paul prayed—but . . . ? It's not an ancient place, and it's not an ancient gospel. It's a place of lighted lamps, and girded loins, where God meets a man's swift hope, and outruns it!

THE MYSTERIES OF THE CROSS

*And when they were come to the place which is called
Calvary, there they crucified him.*

LUKE xxiii:33

THE story of the Cross is told quite simply in the gospels, with very little attempt at description, and one might almost say with no attempt whatsoever at explanation. It looks like no more than the inevitable sequel—well, to the Sermon on the Mount: the only kind of thing that could ever have happened to God among men!

And yet—I confess to you that I can no longer approach it without the sense not of tragedy so much as of unfathomable mystery. It can still be told simply, but it cannot even now be simply catalogued and simply dismissed. It will not allow you to stop thinking about it, as though you were quite content with what you had seen and understood. It keeps haunting you with the suggestion of undiscovered and untraversed meanings. And it's these mysteries of the cross that bring men back to it forever.

To begin with, it keeps relating itself in some unaccountable fashion to the mystery of sin. When Socrates drinks his hemlock, you think somehow of truth and the heroism of men who are willing to die for it; when Jesus is nailed fast to these two rough beams of wood, you think somehow as the centuries have thought: of human sin and the only blow that ever has been struck clean at its roots. And that thought of yours isn't just the flower of an ancient tradition, growing, blossoming through the years: it's a conviction that sprang full-blown from the very inmost circle of the Saviour's own familiar and bosom friends! The little group standing around the philosopher's bed in Athens watching a man die by inches was sure when it was over that the world was forever poorer by one great soul; death had had to do with Socrates. The death on Calvary had to do with sin, and the men who stood afar off watching Jesus die came boldly to proclaim that the world was eternally richer for it! There's no parallel for that in history; where dying has been common, for one Man's death to tower like this into a refuge!

A refuge from the only thing that ever has harassed human life beyond endurance. You can refuse to think about sin if you want to, but you can never get away from having to deal with it. Underneath all the changes that are made from time to time in our philosophy, underneath all the varying fashions that conduct seems to take from generation to generation, there it is. And nobody much outside of a pulpit has anything to say about it. A good many who are inside refer to it only indirectly and with apologies to our superficial and shallow-minded times. While the world goes on dying of the thing! A thousand books that are supposed to help you learn how to live never come to the point. They are just about as appropriate as drinking a toast to a man with the death-rattle in his throat! Sometimes you feel like running your fingers through your hair and crying aloud, "God in Heaven, will nobody say anything?"

But not only is sin persistent in spite of the way in which we try to ignore it; it's dreadful. People doctor it up and make plays out of it for an evening's amusement. They put good clothes on it and write a novel, in which, as Channing Pollock has pointed out, it's smart to be dirty, and cynical, and disregardful of everything upon which every decent civilization has to be founded and by means of which this civilization of ours must endure, if it does endure.

Even you and I frequently enough regard the whole thing with precious little concern. We condone it in ourselves, and sometimes shake our heads with secret admiration for the men and women who seem to get away with it, as we say, in the grand manner: who covet largely, and cheat broadly, and murder magnificently in armies! While by reason of it all, what we call society is crumbling in front of our eyes. It's the only thing in the whole wide world that makes our going difficult! People who spend their time being afraid of disease and poverty and loneliness and pain are "fools and blind" to pass sin by with nothing but a shrug. When a man once really sees how life is, he'll get down on his knees and make a prayer of that cry: "God in Heaven, will nobody say anything?"

The mystery of it is that two thousand years ago one Man did say something by dying; and there's still nothing else to be said!

The night before, in Gethsemane, he trembled; and it wasn't at death. Of that I'm sure. He was no coward, less brave than the women and children who have since died for him. It isn't human weakness you stumble on in the prayer he prayed, Father, if it be thy will let this cup pass from me; and in the sweat that was like great drops of blood. That's not the slack in the fibre of a man's courage: that's the tautness in God's face staring without any veil into the abyss of human sin; it's the tortured knowledge of God standing on the brink of its own appalling leap to get under the farthest estate to which any soul can fall! As the eagle is said to dart with the swiftness of the wind to spread her wings beneath her fledgling when it drops. Father, if it be Thy will—and then to walk off, with eyes wide open as he did, into the yawning mouth of the Thing!

That's one of the mysteries of the cross, that in some unaccountable way it has got itself related to the eternal, caustic, mordant mystery, for all our attempts to gloss it over, of human sin! And it brings me to another: that in some fashion, equally unaccountable, it has got itself related to the eternal, triumphant mystery of human assurance in the face of that sin! I do not know how it happened, and no one else does. The theories about it have never satisfied anybody very long. It's the fact that interests and concerns me. And that fact simply stated is just this: that the only complete and final answer to the riddle of lust and greed and selfishness and injustice and cruelty which life has ever discovered, it has found on Calvary. Nowhere else have men learned to stand as straight and look so steadily into those evil eyes with as little terror. It's what George Matheson meant in his hymn, O Cross, that liftest up my head. If ever there was a place on this green earth where a man's head should be bowed down, it's in front of that desolate cross! And it has come to be the one place on earth where he has a right to lift it!

Here is the mystery of assurance; and it's rooted I think in the sublime and bewildering confidence of Christ himself. You would have called those hours on Calvary an end, and he went into them as though they were really just the beginning, and almost all of it was beyond. He wasn't harried, as a man is whose plans are being brought to exactly nothing; he was quiet and sure-footed, like a man who knows his way through! Peace I leave with you. My peace

I give unto you. The author of the epistle to the Hebrews has caught the plodding certainty of his soul: who for the joy that was set before him endured the cross, despising the shame. And Major Todd has caught it in one of his paintings. There on the cross hangs the limp, torn body of the Crucified, but moving out from it in the radiant manhood of an eternal purpose forever being fulfilled, comes toward you the triumphant Christ of Galilee!

Calvary just doesn't make sense until you come to call it a victory! You can begin to piece it together then, and the odd conduct of one in the flower of his youth calling out to a silent God, It is finished; Father, into Thy hands I commend my spirit! He wasn't losing anything that day, not even his life: he was winning something—and something that men have gone away with in their hearts ever since, whispering to themselves, hardly daring to say it aloud, whispering to themselves, Clean! Looking at the world, and looking at their own soiled lives, as long ago a leper looked at his hands when Jesus had passed and the firm, pink flesh was back, whispering Clean! Clean! So that now, if what you want most in this world is not so much to know as to be known, even loved may be, in spite of what you have been; if you want to do your work and spend your days before some dear Face that's kind, and gracious, and full of tenderness, no matter about the past—why, there you have it. And this is no doctrine men have fashioned; it's an experience they have had. With the cross of Jesus Christ at the centre of it!

That's the second of its mysteries; the mystery of assurance; and here is a third: the mystery of human responsibility. I mean this: You can't leave the cross and live comfortably any more, as if there were nothing left now for anybody else to do! I said a moment ago that the death of Jesus has proved itself the only complete and final answer to the riddle of sin. And it has. You will make no additions to it by anything that you do, nor shall I. And yet—all the strange urgency that stretched out its arms there seems somehow to get down from the cross and lay itself on your own soul! I don't know why or how, but there it is. With everything done for you that can be done, nevertheless you can't sit still and let it go at that! Here is the secret of the power that Calvary has turned loose in the world. Men, real men, just can't look on and go home and get out their slippers and stay comfortably by the fire, and thank God that everything is settled!

Some time ago I was reading a sermon marked by its vigor and the sincerity of its moral passion. The preacher was rebuking that kind of do-less religion which pins its faith to God and never has a single reckless fling of its own for love and justice and mercy and decent human life. Who was it, he asked, who was it wrote

> In the cross of Christ I glory,
> Towering o'er the wrecks of time?

Sir John Bowring. And who was he? He was the British governor-general in Hong Kong at the time when the British Empire was forcing the opium traffic on China, and he was the agent of that policy. Startled that such a hymn could live side by side with such a job, I got hold of the only sketch I could find of Sir John's life, and there I read the nine-tenths which the preacher didn't tell, his distinguished career, his philanthropies, his reforms, the lives he launched into public usefulness, the high service he rendered between nations; and I won back my love for his hymn. The man who wrote it hadn't betrayed it so whole-heartedly as that: he couldn't!

And who, went on the preacher—who wrote

> How sweet the name of Jesus sounds
> In a believer's ear?

John Newton. And who was he? He ran a slave ship between Africa and the slave markets of the western world. Every Sunday he read the church liturgy to his crew twice, in the morning and at even-song, with the moans and the stench of a doomed humanity boiling up into his ears and nostrils out of the ship's hold. So I went back to the life of John Newton, and I read the pitiful story of his long struggle to be rid of that vicious self which he had come increasingly to hate; and I read of how he wrote his hymn twenty-one years after he had become a minister of the Church of England! It wasn't fair to say such things of him! His epitaph which he himself wrote, set down at last in stone, records his own glad and solemn confession:

JOHN NEWTON, Clerk,
Once an Infidel and Libertine,
A servant of slaves in Africa,
Was, by the rich mercy of our Lord and Saviour
JESUS CHRIST
Preserved, restored, pardoned,
And appointed to preach the Faith
He had long laboured to destroy.

And I went back to his hymn from the preacher who had done him so much unkindness! He too had not betrayed what he had seen nor got away from it long. No man can, when once it gets hold, no real man! Not long!

So I say the story can still be told simply: When they were come to the place called Calvary, there they crucified him. But it cannot even now be simply dismissed. It keeps haunting you with the sense of undiscovered worlds, as if you had never really quite seen or understood it: the dark, mordant mystery of sin, persistent and dreadful; the mystery of triumphant assurance, lifting up its head in that most desolate spot with the light of God's mercy on it; and this last, which I think is the greatest mystery of all, that I, being myself but a poor object of his grace, am nevertheless one other hope, one other chance God has for his world!

NOW ABOUT THE CHURCH

NOW, about the Church. There are few issues today which seem more vital. In Germany it's the relation of the Church to the State that keeps thrusting itself every other Tuesday into the spotlight of world news. In Great Britain and here in America it's the relation of the Church to the seething ferment of social and economic unrest which disturbs us and threatens to become the turning point of many a bitter controversy. While on every side the increasing concern for religion and the good life brings more and more into the focus of attention this seemingly divided, certainly bewildered body of would-be disciples called the Christian Church. History has more than once been compelled to make terms with it. It has come through persecutions, the collapse of empires, the assaults of philosophy and science. Now at the centre of the human epic it stands up again, a strangely moving and undaunted will in the world that refuses to leave sin and death alone. Once more history must make terms with it. It isn't inappropriate that we should set down here at the last as clearly as we can, for what it's worth, the terms of our faith in the Church.

If I were asked why I believe in it as passionately as I do, my first answer would be, because it's the only institution I know which with its parishes and its schools stands year in and year out, century upon century, for a religious view of life. Its faults are known to me. More than anything else of course they are the faults of people like us who are its members. You will find them in abundance wherever human beings gather, though fewer of them in the Church I dare say than out of it! With regard to its organization, frankly, I have found it many a time to be considerably more efficient than some of the business concerns which like to criticize it for its incompetence, better able to carry on its work under reduced circumstances, making one dollar go farther and be happier than any two elsewhere, quietly winning its way with a younger generation, often enough in spite of the parents, and not spending a fortune on advertising to do any of it! But all this aside. Even if the Church were what some men keep saying it is, full of hypocrisy, and with no more aptness for affairs than an elderly gentlewoman in a faint—still I should be for it, and simply on this basis: that by its very genius persistently and unequivocally it continues to insist on a religious reading of the world and of human life. Nothing else does. And we can't afford to dispense with that reading! It's the Church, and the Church alone, that lifts our ponderous earth to its ear, as we would lift a shell, and hears the roll of an eternal sea!

What does it mean to have one permanent witness raising its voice against all the accumulated despair of a disillusioned age, against that defeat of man's spirit which is the most appalling hazard of modern times? Here for instance is Mark Twain's cynical appraisal of life: "A myriad of men are born; they labor and sweat and struggle for bread; they squabble and scold and fight; they scramble for little mean advantages over one another. Age creeps upon them. Infirmities follow. Those they love are taken from them. Until at length ambition is dead; pride is dead; longing for release is in their place. It comes at last—the only unpoisoned gift earth ever had for them—and they vanish from a world where they were of no consequence." Life to him seemed a profitless road, an arid path through a desert, a "futility so prolonged and complicated and diabolical as to be worse than absurd." What is it worth to have one permanent witness forever and forever saying "No" to that, recalling human life to the mysteries beyond its sight?

What is it worth to have one permanent witness holding out for it that life is purposeful; that our being here means something, and means something portentous and eternal; that through defeat and all seeming futility and death a power far greater than our own is making on this earth for righteousness; that in a world where we have suddenly begun to think of human life as cheap, the human soul is still the one inconceivably precious thing, with its dreams and its visions and its powers and its destiny? What does it mean to have one institution at least believing in that soul's limitless possibilities of recovery and triumph, believing in its ultimate mastery over all the brutal forces of existence? About twenty-five years ago the Titanic sank. Shortly after, one of our American newspapers carried two drawings. One was of the giant liner ripped open like a fragile toy, and underneath was the caption, The Weakness of Man, the Supremacy of Nature. By its side was the other drawing. It was the likeness of a certain distinguished passenger stepping back to give his place in the last life-boat to a woman and her child. Underneath it was the caption, The Weakness of Nature, the Supremacy of Man. What is it worth to have one voice left asserting that supremacy, whatever happens, and never letting go? Not a university nor a college, save those that belong to the Church; no insurance company, no business enterprise, no laboratory, no science: the Church is all that's left contending for the meaningfulness of life, for the sovereign dignity of man, and for the integrating reality of religious faith. I believe in it because I believe that the world can't get along without the convictions it keeps alive.

Then too I believe in the Church because it's the only institution on earth dedicated to the worship of God. I am not talking now of its divine origin; I am talking only of the indispensable and incalculable service it renders human life. And this is the second. It keeps alive the spirit of worship. Worship is not a luxury; it's a necessity. Said an African chief once, We know that at night-time Somebody goes by among the trees, but we never speak of it. The Church is the only institution on earth that does speak of it, and goes on, beyond speaking, to beckon men into the awe and majesty of his Presence, who went by once in a still small voice, in the crying of prophets, in an angels' song, and a cross, and a broken tomb; who lifts a challenge in our conscience, as another has put it, and gleams in our compassion like a candle lit on a high altar.

Mankind's belief in that Other is as inevitable as breathing. We find ourselves in a world where we cannot help reaching out and up. In Robert Louis Stevenson's *Ebb Tide* Herrick resolves to let himself down into the water and drown, but finds that he can't stop swimming. Instinct compels him to keep moving his hands and his feet. So Job, though quite sure that God's against him, cannot keep from praying, and accounts for his conduct by asking, Doth not one stretch out his hand in his fall? So inevitable is it. As when Leslie Stephen wrote of his wife, after her death, "I thank—" and then remembered he had no God, and went on, "I thank—something—that I loved her as heartily as I know how to love." That "something"—him to whom life turns and will not be denied—that Someone in the dawn, and the spring, and the sound of laughter, and the silent falling of tears—him the Church proclaims. Nothing else does. In a world where Voltaire said if there were no God we should have to invent him, in such a world the Church alone calls the human soul to its solemn salutation in the presence of the divine. I believe in the Church because I believe we can't dispense with that.

Worship is the most poignant need of the soul. The word itself is nothing but the old English worth-ship. It's the natural acknowledgment of eternal worth. It's the normal moving about with hushed lips under the great dome of the sky, and a growing the taller for it. But more than anything else I think, it's the haunting sense of ultimate good back of all the sorrows and pain and black darkness of life. The story is told of a lad, wounded to death in the Great War an hour or two before the Armistice, all his cherished hopes of home and loved ones broken at the last moment, that as he lay there dying and heard for the first time the longed-for news of peace, he whispered with his last breath, more to himself than to any one else, Isn't it just like God to do a thing like this? Christian worship is a quiet stealing away in the company of Christ from all such "pitiful and desolating ignorance" to One who even at the foot of a cross—aye, and on it—is to be trusted utterly: Father, into thy hands I commend my spirit. Worship is the deep knowledge that behind the broken body of Jesus, as in one stirring canvas of the crucifixion, are the hands and feet of God, pierced by the nails, too, but God still, vast and triumphant! Worship is the sure assertion that underneath all the hurried writing on the surface of life is another writing, ancient and not beyond deciphering: and that writing runs, The goodness of God endureth continually!

We go to church week after week to say that to one another, and to bow our heads as the sign of his coming among us. And about it all, to enrich our being there, about the hymns we sing and the prayers our lips form, is the wealth of ten thousand years: poor blind folk of the dim past kneeling before their cruel gods; austere folk marching highly out of Egypt toward the desert and the East; then one day a gentle youth at a carpenter's bench, and such words as never yet man spake; a bitter hour on Calvary; a breathless moment in a garden; the long years with their thin red line of martyrs; the gaunt faith of crusader and scholar and monk—all this, with the sound of their muffled voices, to enrich our being there— voices that keep with ours, chanting Holy, Holy, Holy, Lord God of Hosts! I believe that when a man turns his back on that, on these places and these hours which seem to shine with all the light of sacred story—I believe that then the spirit of worship slowly dies within him. And I believe that when that happens, there is nothing left on earth that's worth to him the pain of living! I believe that worship does something for him that nothing else can do. It satisfies him, and cleanses him, and frees him from himself, and knits up the broken fragments of his life, and lifts his face undaunted again to the hills! That's why I believe in the Church. First, because it stands alone for a religious view of life. Second, it stands alone for the worship of God.

And now third! I believe in the Christian Church because it's the only institution on earth that's given over to the realization here and now of the mind and spirit and will of Jesus Christ. It doesn't have any notable resources, not visibly at least. One is appalled at their meagreness. Here are some facts. Look at this for instance. In the last five years the average of our national income has increased more than fifty per cent. Of that income twice as much as before has gone into cars, and three times as much into alcohol. Some industries have multiplied themselves by forty! But for every dollar of income that the Protestant Church had five years ago, she has seventy cents now. The total of her revenues seems to be a little over a third of what we are spending at the moment on armaments. It's just a third of what we are spending on motion pictures. As regards cigarettes, we are not so badly off: they get only twice as much! I wonder sometimes what could really be done if we weren't all bled to death for these other things! And so had enough to spread ourselves a little when it comes to the things that are really basic in our civilization!

No, the Church isn't very adequately supplied. Nobody ever thinks of supporting it, with its schools, its colleges, its works of mercy—nobody but the members; and we either can't—which is true of many—or we won't—which is true of others! At least not in any measure that answers at all to its importance.

And yet it goes on steadily doing what it can to bring the Kingdom of God on the earth! Nothing else aims in that direction. The Church at least aims. One of the speakers at Town Hall not so long ago was deploring our common American notion of success. He said he had seen pictures of it in magazines, a man sitting at a desk with a row of push-buttons in front of him—I neglected to remark that the desk was mahogany! He said, this speaker, that he had more than once caught the echo of that struggle after money and power in the advice given by parents to their children. He had heard its beginnings in university corridors, and been startled by its syllables from the Christian pulpit. So he said. Now in my day I have listened to a good many sermons, as have some of you; but I have yet to hear in any church from any pulpit, good, bad, or indifferent, that gospel preached! I have heard there the only corrective for it! The Christian Church, as nothing else, has kept setting another dream in the hearts of men, until here today and yonder tomorrow, somebody gets on his feet and fashions some mercy, some clean justice, into fact, some hope that Christ had let wistfully into his life. That's how all the good there is in the world found its way out of the love of God into human history! There's no doubt about it at all—back of our social agencies and those that contribute to them, back of the forces working for world peace, for the care of the sick and the relief of the poor, back of the steady drive for righteousness in government and in industry, is the Christian Church, as the spring is back of the river, trying to give the mind of Christ its way in the world, sending about their daily tasks among men such freedom and brotherhood and tenderness as we have!

That's why I believe in it, because I am in debt to it as I am in debt to no other institution in the world; and so is the whole round sum of human life, whether men acknowledge the debt or not. I believe in it because I believe that today it's pouring into our cities and into this nation a mighty stream of faith and hope and love without which both our civic and our national well-being would be set in the most instant jeopardy. In short I believe in the Christian Church because I believe that nothing else on earth will ever take over its work, or do it half so well! I believe in the Christian Church. Do you? If you do, then live it! And may God keep your faith in muscle and give it hands!